It Doesn't Matter Which Road You Take

A European Travel Story

By Vincent Yanez

PublishAmerica
Baltimore

ISBN: 1-60441-468-5
PUBLISHED BY PUBLISHAMERICA, LLLP
www.publishamerica.com
Baltimore

Printed in the United States of America

This book is dedicated to my travel-chum, Chris, for your patience, your meticulous notes and the fact that you saved the world on at least three separate occasions.
Without you, this book would only be half as thick.

ACKNOWLEDGEMENTS

To begin with, *Thank You* to the guys at **bootsnall.com**, who first published my story and got it out into the travel-story world. To **Babak Fakhamzadeh,** who turned my story into a beautiful online work of art for **travelhog.net** (see his work on babakfakhamzadeh.com). Also, to places like authorsden.com and hostels.com, for keeping online travel writing alive.

To my fellow authors at bootsnall, Christine Michaud, Keiron Burchell and Craig Guillot who are doing the type of writing I hope to someday aspire to (check them out at bootsnall.com). *Thank you* also to ma and pa, who have put up with my constant 'picking up and moving' and have always been supportive of every mistake I make, be it *poco* or *grande*.

And a big *Thank You* to the Continent of Europe, for letting us come over and loiter. God knows Americans aren't exactly the most popular people in the world, so we tried not to litter, talk too loudly or generally make a bad impression. Hopefully we represented well. Lastly, and quite fondly, to Bishinik, my little bird of happiness.

Prologue

4 a.m.

The door to our compartment flies open and two men in dark blue uniforms push their way in. *"Pas prosim vás!"*

We hand over our passports and Eurail passes. The younger of the two takes them and begins flipping through the pages. He says something to the older man whose glare ensures that we will most likely be thrown from the moving train into the pitch black of the Czech countryside within the hour. The younger one unfolds our Eurail map and points out to me what should be obvious. This is not a valid document to enter their country. The Czech Republic is not included in the train pass we had purchased a month earlier. I feign my surprise.

Chris gives me one of those looks. If we make it to see one more morning, he's going to kill me. It isn't exactly my fault we have gotten caught. To his credit, he did bring to light that our train passes do not cover traveling through the Czech Republic. I believe I reasoned that it was a non-stop night train and who would be paying that close attention anyway?

The older gentleman suddenly leaves the compartment in what seems like a rush. The younger of the two tucks our passports into his front coat pocket. He looks at each of us and smiles. *"Bude to trvat moment."* It will be just a moment.

CHAPTER ONE

Departure to Europe

Turbulence, Large Craniums and Moving Sidewalks

When I announce I want to go to Europe, I am not surprised by anyone's response. My siblings take it in stride as just another *Vince thing*. My boss gives me a hundred and fifty bucks, a copy of Michener's The Drifters, and the address for a Biergarten in Munich. My parents do not object, they only think it would be wiser if I use my newly acquired degree to find a stable, well-paying job and then work towards a nice two-week vacation that will ensure I have both money and employment to come back to. Of course, at this point in their lives, neither has been to Europe…so this I take with a grain of salt.

My friends understand my need to wander. We have all been milling about in a fog of uncertainty since the day our university handed us our diplomas and told us to get the hell out. They see this as just a way of me saying I have no idea what to do with my life. This is not altogether inaccurate. They are just as lost.

I ask my best friend, Chris, if he wants to go. We are complete opposites.

He is anal, orderly and not very good under pressure. I am lax, messy and do not normally show signs of stress. He is enthusiastic to travel. He too is facing the same goal-less future.

Neither of us has traveled much, unless you count the cross-country trips we made to see how far our cars would go. The only other country he has visited is Canada, which is not really much of another country; it's more like a higher version of America. I have only been just over the Mexican border, and spent so much time with a guy name Jose Cuervo, reminiscence of these trips would be somewhat inaccurate. We embrace this opportunity to open our eyes, add to our gray matter, stimulate our taste buds and improve our postures.

I am planning on a three-month trip, though neither of us has much in the way of money. After deducting the cost of plane and train tickets, I have seven hundred dollars in cash and a credit card that is itching to be used. Chris only has a bit more.

We need luggage. The backpacks we like are huge, green things and the salesman says that they are big enough for a small woman to fit inside. Neither of us is planning on picking up any small women, but the salesman convinces us that we never really know what we might want to bring back. The bottom of the pack expands to give us an extra foot of packing space, should we need it. I suppose this would be useful if the small woman wants to stretch.

These bags are scientifically constructed to ensure the weight of its content rests on specific pressure points. The metal framing sewn inside is to keep our spines from snapping during a slight breeze. However, what wins are hearts and our pocketbooks, is the small backpack that detaches from the large one. It looks like a little pod coming off the mother ship. We have to have these bags.

Packing seems harder than it should be. The only reason my clothes fit is because I discover the trick of rolling my garments into a sort of log shape, and then stacking these 'logs' into the bag. Folding took up too much space. Stuffing everything haphazardly almost worked, but the clothes came out looking like a car had run me over and dragged me forty yards. Rolling is fun, easy, and gives everything that freshly rolled look. I am able to take more than I had originally thought, thus I will not have to wear the same shirt fourteen days in a row.

Chris is somehow able to fit a lot more into his bag. This makes me jealous at first, and then I try to lift his bag, and walk away chuckling softly to myself. He has brought along enough sweaters to ward off the slightest change in temperature. He also found a way to fit in an extra pair of shoes. I have to wonder if the nearly busting look is a good way for his bag to start the trip. Of course I poke fun at him, to which he replies that he plans on leaving his old things behind as he picks up new ones. It would be great if we could do that with every aspect of our lives.

We sit down with a map to plot our journey. My only request is that even though we are making an itinerary, we leave it loose enough to be able to take things as they pop up. Chris says, "Of course we will." Something tells me he may be humoring me. I have already found that he has made a list of every item contained within his backpack, including the number of Q-tips he is carrying.

Everything is working out fine until Chris starts to refer to his need for 'closure'. We have decided to fly into London, tour Great Britain, cross the Channel and then do the mainland of Europe. I figure this way, at the end of our journey, we would fly out of a main airport like Paris or Rome. Makes perfect sense to me.

Chris, on the other hand, decides that at the end of the trip we should schlep our way back to London and fly out of the same airport we flew into. He draws me a diagram on a map that shows us landing in London, doing Europe and then flying out of London. He points to the neat circle this makes.

I point out that not only will it take us two or three days to get back to England, but God knows how much more it will cost us to re-cross the English Channel and taxi our way into London. This does not matter to him. My way is the way of the Neanderthals. It offers no sense of completion. It provides nothing that resembles the visual treat of his well-drawn circle on the map, and worst of all; it provides him with no closure.

We argue back and forth about closure and how important it is in one's life and/or travels. He is shocked at my inability to see the poetry in it all. I am unable to explain to him that closure is something you aim for in relationships and unexpected deaths, not backpacking trips. He's getting on my nerves and we haven't even left yet. Much more of this and I'll pop a blood vessel in my left eye.

Sadly and most regrettably, when the time comes to purchase our airline tickets, Chris is unable to meet me at the travel agent's office. As I sit in the waiting area, alone, I try to represent his argument. But, alas, in the end there must be a victor. The result of his plea for closure, poetry and completion is made apparent on our airline tickets. We are flying into London and out of Paris. Voila!

We both move out of our apartments in Tucson. He goes home to Prescott and I go home to Globe. On April the 18th we meet at Phoenix International Airport to begin our European Expedition.

Our flight from Phoenix to Cincinnati is as uneventful as any flight to Cincinnati most likely is. Chris plays with the air vents and periodically points out that the safety seal on the exit door is broken. The turbulence is bad and I make Jurassic Park references with my bouncing cup of soda. He eats his pack of peanuts and loudly enjoys his Ginger Ale. We make bets on who will lose their luggage first, but to our surprise, both bags make the first leg of our trip. Of course, this makes us cocky and carefree.

The next leg of our journey is Cincinnati to London. Thirty minutes into our flight and I hear a strange banging noise from the back of the plane. My audio senses are rewarded as the captain announces we have to land. He explains that, due to a break in the seal of our cargo bay door, we are flying to the nearest airport for repairs. I prepare for a rapid loss of cabin pressure or a sudden steep dive to our deaths, but the rest of the plane seems unconcerned as the stewardess begins to pass out refreshments. As a precaution, I remain in a slightly stooped position, ready to grab my ankles and pray.

We seem to be flying a bit fast for such a large, airborne object with a door slightly ajar. A look out the window shows that we have dropped our elevation enormously as we fly into Tennessee. I can not only see the rooftops of the town below us with great clarity, but we are so low, I can tell the difference between a porch light and a bug-zapper. I wave to a small boy playing in his back yard. He waves back.

We land safely in Tennessee. They inform us that it will take only a moment to fix and that we will not be disembarking the airplane. Five minutes later they inform us that it will in fact take two hours to fix, and we will not be disembarking the plane. Though they are not allowing us to vacate this hell and go someplace more comfortable, like a shoebox, they are going to reward our imprisonment with the early distribution of our dinner and the showing of our in-flight movie.

Our dinner is the lovely choice of Southwestern Steak Fillet or Herbed Chicken. The smell of this luke-warm delight wafts its way through the cabin and I can't help but finger my vomit bag in anticipation. The movie they are showing is something I watched not two weeks ago.

After five minutes of watching Daniel Day-Lewis and Michelle Pfeiffer on a screen the size of stamp, I cannot help but mention the obvious to Chris, movies seem to lose everything when shown on an airplane. He says that he just wants Daniel-Day Lewis and his coy American accent to go away. He then rambles on about how he can't get out of his mind that Michelle Pfeiffer was Catwoman at one point in her career. Apparently, she has ruined all other acting roles for herself as far as Chris is concerned.

The imprisonment is only twenty minutes old and I am starting to become annoyed. The kid in the front row is acting like someone just stabbed him with a fork. At times like this, I wish I had studied Zen or self-hypnosis or the art of the self-inflicted coma, anything to help me escape from this twentieth-century hell we call public transportation. Chris is excited about ordering the Herbed Chicken for dinner.

Two hours later the captain tells us we need to disembark the aircraft. I assume the glue on the newly fixed door did not dry properly and heaven knows the airline does not want to make us any more uncomfortable than we have to be. The flight crew has thoughtfully abandoned us and is most likely either already snuggled in for the night or participating in whatever orgy air travel causes one to participate in. We are left to scramble over our half-eaten trays of food, retrieve our carry-on luggage and make for the exit. The movie rages on.

We are bunched together with our luggage, waiting for the airline to find a place to put us up for the night. Chris has abandoned me, wandering the terminal, looking for something to spend his money on. I spend my time enjoying the company of two lovely southern ladies, Kelley and Shai. Kelley is cute, nice and makes me wish I were more of a stud or at least not so dopey. Shai is nice but seems to be annoyed by everything we are experiencing. If only Chris was near, they could hold a bitch-a-thon.

For some reason the state of Tennessee is unable to provide lodgings for the victims of flight 360. We are shuttled across the state line into Kentucky, to a lovely accommodation that has the unfortunate distinction of trying to look like a medieval castle. The entire flight of one hundred plus passengers is delivered to this Shangri-La by two vans that hold eight people each. Letting the women and children go first, we arrive at the hotel three hours after we got off the plane.

We are given money for room service, but room service stopped servicing two hours ago. Ten minutes in this joint and Chris is annoyed with the castle motif. We go to the attached diner that seems to be a part of the hotel and order enough food to feed a buffalo. What we do not spend of the airline money we give to the waitress as a tip. She is nice and we have taken pity on the fact that she has to serve people who come to a castle hotel intentionally.

A good night's rest and all will be better in the morning. That's what we tell ourselves anyway. God knows what else will happen to us. We are now a day behind on our itinerary, we have not even left American soil and worse yet, we are in a sorta-castle.

The next morning we lounge around the airport waiting for our flight to leave. We are being rerouted to Detroit, at which point we will grab another plane to London. This going up and down in airplanes has got to be bad for us physically. I can only imagine the change in pressure and altitude has formed some sort of air pocket in my brain or something even more horrible. Our boarding gate is A17, but Chris has chosen to sit at gate A15. He says it is providing him with a better summer view.

Chris shares that he feels like he is in the movie Groundhog Day. He says that we are living this day over and over, and that we will never actually get any closer to Europe than we are now. "At least Bill Murray gets the girl at the end of the movie," he tells me. "What do I have? You!"

I tell him I understand his point completely, though part of me just wants to fold up in the corner and weep. I will admit, I am no Andie MacDowell, but I am pretty cute in my torn jeans and over-sized sweatshirt. I sit cross-legged on the floor, close my eyes and put my palms together. If there is a Higher Power, it will get us out of Tennessee.

We meet the girls again and I make it a point to annoy them with my lack of wit and wisdom. Chris watches CNN and learns that the eight octopus tentacles on the ice, at a hockey game, represent the original number of games it took to win the Stanley Cup playoffs. We eventually board the aircraft heading to Detroit, where we will board another aircraft to continue on our European adventure.

We land in Detroit and our luggage is waiting for us, which makes us feel that perhaps we are beginning to push our luck. As we prepare to leave Detroit, for some odd reason we become paranoid that our backpacks may not arrive in London. We convince the stewardess that they are within the carry-on size limit, which is accomplished by some eventual begging on my part. My bag is not actually pushing the regulations too much, but the bag Chris drags on looks like we are transporting cadavers.

We are on our way to Europe. Two hours into our seven-hour flight and I once again detest flying, though this time our airplane cargo door decides to stay on. Dinner has been served. I forgot what I asked for and looking at my meal offers no help as to what I am eating. Airplane food has never impressed me. I do not think they put enough effort into it. I would probably feel this way with any place that would make me eat food that requires the use of utensils in a space that does not even offer enough room to have an eye spasm. We wait for the in-flight movie to begin and I enjoy a handful of free alcoholic beverages.

I make friends with the guy next to me. I feel it is the polite thing to do since our seats are so close together we are probably considered married by Amish standards. He does not seem like a lunatic and I feel it is wise to know the person I could later be using as a flotation device.

Chris is getting frustrated because there is a man, with an enormous head, two rows ahead of him. The sheer mass of it is blocking the movie screen. For a moment it sways out of view and Chris relaxes to enjoy the movie, but then gets twice as mad as the hugely proportioned cranium floats back into view.

With little else to do, Chris decides to converse with me. He tells me how moving sidewalks are one of the greatest inventions of the twentieth century. "They are miracles of modern man," he says. "They make even the clumsiest people seem graceful." We had passed our free time, in the Detroit airport, riding these contraptions. Chris enjoys walking in place. He says it is good exercise. I stand on them to avoid any unsolicited movement.

Another hour goes by before Chris loses his ability to not bitch. He is mad at the space between the seats. He keeps pointing out how much room he *doesn't* have. Due to my Burger King-induced girth, I have to sit with my arms plastered to my sides, like I am sliding down a tube, but it's not about me right now. Chris shifts around and strikes different poses, but less in an effort to get comfortable and more to demonstrate his inability to move any great lengths.

We are two of five people sitting across the middle aisle of the aircraft. We are unlucky enough to be in the center seats, and Chris is finding it difficult to get out and go to the lavatory. He says it might be easier just to urinate in one's seat. He then looks down at his lower regions, contemplates for a moment and then holds his empty cup aloft. "Oh please" he says, directing his speech to the nearest stewardess. "Could I have some more to drink?"

CHAPTER TWO
London

Taco Bell, Knock-Knock Jokes and Lawrence of Arabia

We are almost to London. The excitement on the plane is obvious as everyone shuffles about and wipes themselves down with the moist, microwave-warm hand towels provided by the airline. Chris has pulled out our wish list that he had us write before we left (he likes lists). It contains all the things we think we want to see on our trip. It's not like they are all at the London airport when we land, but it passes the time and draws our attention away from the fact that soon, four-thousand tons of metal is supposed to be put down on a piece of concrete no bigger than a driveway.

My wish list is simple and includes a respectful peek at Van Gogh's grave in Auvers, Vatican City with optional pope-led mass, sitting in a Parisian café at some point and a general want of either falling in love or not getting killed...preferably both.

The list Chris makes is a bit more youthful. He wants to see Agincourt, as his tribute to Kenneth Branagh in the movie Henry V. He also wants to take a stroll through the streets of Prague. He is especially excited to tip his

16

hat at Hemingway's watering hole, Harry's Bar, in Venice, and would like to spend a day at EuroDisney. Of course, these accomplishments are teetering on whether or not they will let me into London.

The plane lands and we are given our freedom. There are things I notice about myself after long, overseas flights. I feel more tired than I should, I become very fond of the ground and I somehow acquire a pungent breath that the boldest of mints cannot extinguish.

The lady in customs decides there is something suspicious about me. Greg (the guy who sat next to me on the plane) and Chris breeze right by her with nothing more than a half-wave. Hell, even the guy with the really big head got through without a problem. Then comes my turn. She has me state my business, asks for my passport, checks through the contents of my backpack, and wants to know how long I am staying and where I plan on residing. The other passengers are watching and a few jeers are tossed as they tell her to leave me be.

My answers don't help her any as they are short and not too well thought out. Chris has the names and addresses of the people and hostels we are planning to stay. I tell her I am just here to wander around for a bit. This answer does not seem to appease her. Maybe she thinks I am being vague. Perhaps she thinks I am a terrorist, with my black hair and cowboy-like stroll. Perhaps my sleepy eyes and denim jacket give me a sinister look. Do I look like the creep that stood her sister up for the prom? I am tired and it takes everything I have not to tell her what a prick she is being. Eventually she grows bored with me and lets me through. I feel sorry for all the puppies she must kick on her way home each day.

We ride the subway, or underground, into Victoria station. Victoria Station is, by far, the coldest structure I had ever set foot in. I could slide down iceberg slopes on my bare bottom and feel warmer than I do now. The high vaulted ceilings and concrete floor offer no resistance to the icy wind blowing through the open doorways along the walls. I am afraid to blink in case my eyelids freeze shut and I think I see a team of sled dogs making their way to a train departing toward Wales.

We pile our bags on the floor. I spread-eagle myself over our belongings as Chris ventures off in search of a bathroom. This became a routine for us in the airports. One person would smother the bags in an attempt to ward off tempted bag smugglers and the other would venture off on some stupid adventure involving either a bathroom or a hot dog. I do not suppose it offers much resistance for anyone who really wants to take our things. However, if they try, I will most likely raise myself from the pile of overstuffed bags, grunting and moaning the whole while, and at least curse in their general direction.

I am getting quite comfy and am near a total jet lag black out when a security guard taps my foot with his club. He informs me that I cannot sit on the floor like this and any bags in the station have to be carried at all times. I understand that there is paranoia of terrorist acts within the city of London, but just one look into my well-meaning eyes should convey that I am not the least bit dangerous. I stare at him with my practiced puppy-dog look. I am hoping to convey to him that most days I have trouble putting on my own wristwatch, much less handle explosive devices. He continues to hover over me so I slowly push myself up like a drunken man.

I contort my body in every angle possible to put the various bag straps wherever is easiest. The security guard stands there, watching me, offering not a bit of help. Does he honestly think I can carry two large backpacks and two smaller backpacks at the same time? I want to smile at him and say something smart, but I am not too sure what it would take to get oneself beaten to death with a club. Chris returns at this moment and interrupts my general cursing of the English and their paranoia. We pile our belongings onto our weary backs and shuffle off down the corridor.

Of course, I realize I have not had my turn at the lavatory, and force him to show me where they are. It costs half a pound to get into the bathroom. Charging me to do my business is one of the most annoying things in the world. Undeniable functions of the body that each of us must adhere to should not be profited from, but then again, I suppose restaurants and brothels would tend to disagree with this type of logic. Restrooms should at least charge you for the type of service you are about to perform, as they are not all the same, but I suppose this would only lead to dishonesty. No, really officer, I was only going to urinate, but then…

The other reason I do not like to have to pay to do my business is because it seems that the places that charge you are usually the ones that have never used a coin to help maintain their particular area in the realm of sanitation. Stepping into this bathroom is like being time-warped back to the days of the Black Plague. There's garbage strewn about, the floors and walls are filthy and there is a man sleeping on the counter above the wash basins. I am afraid to touch anything, much less expose items of my person that may someday bring about a world leader or at least fornicate with one.

I have no desire to take my backpack off again so I have worn it in. I try to get into a stall, but my backpack is too big and I do not fit. Luckily a urinal opens up and I make a dive for it. I have to debate whether or not to wash my hands when I am done. The thought of not washing them disgusts me, but the thought of touching the handle to the sink and taking the risk that the slumbering man may roll over in his sleep and fall on top of me disgusts me a tad more. Luckily, a kind gentleman leaves the faucet on and I do not have to do anything but wet my hands and run for the exit. It puts me in a bad mood to know I paid half a pound to most likely contract some unknown disease. I leave the faucet on and I wonder if the sound of running water is making the homeless guy dream of waterfalls.

We find our hostel on the map and trudge through London's streets, nimbly dodging morning rush hour. The hostel is buried in a grove of trees in the middle of a park. We realize this is supposed to be a serene setting to relax and unwind, but we are both amazed at the seclusion of the place. This would be the perfect setting for a maniac to hack and chop his way through weary travelers without a soul hearing a thing. This makes the walk along our tree-lined path much less enjoyable. We have to wait until three in the afternoon to get in our room. The beds cost us thirty-three dollars each and the key deposit is another thirty (refundable) dollars. A sheet and pillow will be extra.

One of the exciting things we heard before we left was how the hostels would only cost us eight to ten dollars a night. This is true in some remote hostels in the middle of dilapidated rain forests. Other than that, most hostels in and around major European cities, subsequent to 1978, charge almost as much as cheap hotels. We dump our backpacks and are thankful that they do not ask us for a holding fee. Gathering our guidebooks, we set out to wander the streets of London.

We are both grumpy and I am extremely jet-lagged. If I was not so tired we would probably be arguing right now, but luckily, lack of sleep has eased my nerves. We make it back to Victoria Station to try and figure out what to do on our first day. The thought of a London-version of a Broadway play seems intriguing, but the price of a ticket would take a large chunk of our money and I can guarantee that I will be asleep by the middle of the first act. We decide to jump on one of the red double-decker buses in front of the station. It's time for a hop-on hop-off tour.

For the common tourist, these bus tours are the greatest invention since Pepto-Bismol. They drive all over their respective city, pointing out all the major tourist attractions and allowing you to jump on or off whenever the fancy strikes you. Unfortunately, the feeling of a seat beneath my butt causes my body to finally succumb to the jet lag, and not ten minutes into our tour I fall sound asleep. I awaken to the sound of the bus pulling back in to Victoria Station. My first tour of London looked exactly like the back of my eyelids. The tour guide takes pity on us and gives us a ticket to ride again tomorrow for free. Being as tired as I am I almost want to weep and hug the nice man. Instead I just give him an award-winning smile.

Of course, now I feel like someone has run me over and I am hungry to boot. We wander the streets thinking we will find some fish and chips, shepherd's pie or something else incredibly English. As luck would have it, there is not a chip in sight. We end up giving in to our American stupidity and eating a wonderfully disgusting meal of Big Macs and fries at the local McDonald's.

I feel nauseated and the food doesn't help. We go back to the hostel. Our room is like a dorm with eight other beds strewn about. The shower is communal, as is the bathroom. Chris hates roughing it, and to him, this constitutes roughing it. I only want to go to sleep.

Chris is considering a trip to the front desk to ask if we can have a private room. Normally I would make some lewd comment as to what exactly his intentions are toward me, but I am too tired to be obnoxious. He says that he can explain our flying difficulties, my bus-induced coma and my talking in my sleep.

Apparently, while staying in our medieval hotel in Kentucky, I was talking all night about plane tickets, boarding passes, seat numbers and departure times. Though I appear almost annoyingly calm in the face of crises, it all comes out in a mad anxious rush while I am sleeping. Of course, the part that made him most annoyed was the fact that he stood awake that night trying to answer my, as he put it, random, frantic ravings. We decide to just tough it out and I am asleep by six in the afternoon.

I awaken refreshed and alert. The sun is just starting to work its way through the partially open window, a slight breeze is toying with the lace curtain and I can hear the sound of birds singing. I am excited to introduce myself to this place called London. I look at my alarm clock and see that it is five-thirty in the morning. This is appalling, no one should be awake this early unless they are delivering milk or in the military. I lie back down and eventually drift off to sleep. Half an hour later, Chris coming back from the shower awakens me. I have a headache and my neck hurts. This is more like it.

We vote to get the hell out of this hostel. I figure it will be cheaper to drink ourselves silly in a pub or at least find a run down B&B to crash in. We go to Victoria Station in hopes of finding something that looks like directions to lodgings. The fact that everything is written in English does not go unappreciated. Chris is approached by a guy handing out brochures for a youth hostel, which makes us leery, but this is only due to the fact that we are both paranoid.

We are milling around for a bit, letting the early morning chill of the station work its way to our bone marrow, when a man and woman approach us. They are wearing backpacks similar to ours, which immediately makes them part of the brotherhood. The man tells us that the place to stay is called the Chelsea Hotel. He says there is a booth outside of the station and the rates are good.

Outside we find the booth, occupied by a woman reading a magazine. We tell her what we want and she makes a phone call. Ten minutes later a little van screeches to the curb. She tells us to get inside and he will take us to the hotel. Chris and I look at each other. Rule number two, when growing up, was never get in a car with a stranger. Rule number one was all about not taking candy from them, but who are we kidding, if he were to offer me a candy bar at this moment I would probably take it.

We stick our heads in the window and take a good look at the driver.

He looks like a reincarnation of a young John Lennon. Round spectacles, mop of hair, wiry build and wearing a sleeveless shirt with the word LOVE written across it. We decide we can physically overpower this hippie if we have to and clamor into the van. He is a nice enough fellow and proceeds to tell us about the hotel as he drives 180 miles an hour through the streets of London.

I compliment him on narrowly missing both pedestrians and other cars, and what is meant to be sarcasm is taken as a compliment. He thanks me and explains that he is studying to be a taxi driver. He says that it takes up to five years to get a taxi license in London. There are so many streets with the same name, like Chester Lane, Boulevard, Way, Street, Hill, Knoll and Avenue, and each of these may at one time or another intersect with another one. The roads are mostly paved over mud paths that were originally used by coaches to get through the city, and you can tell their designs seem to have been made more by meandering horses rather than engineers.

I am developing a tumor from watching the scenery zoom by at near light speed and my right leg hurts from stomping on the floorboard every time I think braking would be a good idea. We screech to a halt in front of the hotel. As I tumble out of the van, I have to force myself not to drop to my knees and kiss the ground. He says he will wait for us as we check out the hotel.

On the way up the stairs, Chris wants to know what will happen if we decide not to stay at this hotel. He is thinking we should not say anything that would upset Mr. Lennon if we plan on getting back into his brake-impaired vehicle. I guess we can take a room no matter what the price, or sneak out the back entrance and run.

Luckily, the Chelsea Hotel is a wonderful place and the rates are reasonable. Chris is excited that we are given a room of our own and does a happy dance when he finds that we even have our own bathroom. We drop our bags in the room and chuckle at the sink next to the tub. It is in perfect shape except for a large whole, about the size of my head, at the bottom of it. Luckily, the missing piece is lying near the sink, and with some patience, the whole thing fits back together quite nicely.

The young John Lennon offers to take us back to Victoria Station and we accept. Our travel guide lists that cabbies in England are not normally tipped. We find this quite odd and it feels weird not tipping. In America, failing to tip a taxi driver will most certainly result in your learning a few new words for genitalia. When we arrive at our destination, we each give him a handful of coinage that seems to please him quite a bit. I am wondering if perhaps we are part of a small minority that tips their drivers. Chris is thinking maybe we figured out the money thing wrong and we just paid that man enough to re-enroll in university.

We decide to use our hop-on, hop-off tickets today. A red double-decker bus pulls up and we happily jump aboard. Our first stop is Piccadilly Circus, which I decide is the Times Square of London. Chris is amazed at the size of the posters advertising mediocre American movies. I cannot get over the number of pretty women we see walking by. Is everyone here really this beautiful or if I am just worked up? I assume a little of both. We go to Leicester Square and drink cappuccinos.

Chris tells me to imagine that all the girls are wearing riding crops and this does not help my situation. Chris says that even without fanaticizing about horse-riding clothes, the English are quite fashionable. I make a societal statement; the English are too fashion conscious, and not conscious enough about anything else. I am not too sure what it means exactly, but it sounds important at the time.

We go to Tower Records and I happily build a pile of videos that I have never been able to find in America. Of course, Chris bursts my bubble of joy by pointing out that they will not play in our American VCR's. He then struts to the Imported CD section and finds that all it contains is overpriced CDs imported from America. As the smile leaves his face I feel somehow vindicated.

We walk on to Trafalgar Square and watch the pigeons do whatever it is pigeons do. They are all waddling around looking for a handout. If people stopped feeding them, the little beggars would probably fly away, but the tourists are throwing out breadcrumbs by the handful. There are hundreds of them and some are as big as dachshunds. I hope everyone does not act surprised when one of these feathery rags decides to walk off with a small child for its lunch. I find them to be disgusting but Chris is amused. He informs me that he thinks he was a pigeon in a past life because of the way he moves his head back and forth when he rides in cars.

Chris wants pictures with the pigeons and he also wants to sit on the giant lions that are ceremoniously draped with tourists, pigeons and bird shit. I convince him that this is an unoriginal idea and there are too many people around to make the picture worthwhile. The reason he is so interested in this monument is because it is the symbol of Nelson Entertainment, the distributor of such films as When Harry Met Sally and The Princess Bride. He eventually agrees to forego this dream and I can only imagine the diseases we have managed to avoid thus far.

We wander over to the National Gallery and I am nearly dancing in my shoes. I find myself staring up at Van Gogh's Chair and the Pipe, Lilies, Park and Hills with Cypress Trees. Chris finds himself in a room next to a woman who uses the word bum. She says something about how the artist has painted the bum, and he has to stifle his guffaw as he quickly exits the room. Americans are idiots sometimes, we know.

After staring at the Cezanne's, Gaugan's, Monet's and Manet's we look at the Horse Guards, then stroll over to Number 10 Downing Street. I am very impressed at how normal this residence appears. I wonder if it is as easy to stroll up to the door and knock as it seems to be. I contemplate doing this for a bit until I convince myself that somewhere, across the street, is a member of the English Secret Service who has had too many crumpets, too few bathroom breaks and is now watching me through the eye piece of his rifle. I walk on.

I am wondering what time it is, so we wander over to Big Ben. We have both seen pictures of this, but the real thing is beyond what we could have imagined. I find it incredibly useful in answering my question of the time of day. As we reach the corner of Westminster and Victoria, (at least this is where Chris says we are. I am lucky if I know what city I am in, much less the street I am on), Big Ben strikes five o'clock. The bongs are big and deep and career off the city walls. It is an amazing thing to witness and we are giddy for minutes afterward.

We arrive at Westminster Abbey. Chris is becoming very impressed by this whole architecture thing. The gothic-ness, the stone walls, stained glass windows, arches, pillars and the whole package. He says the buildings of today are crappy and uninspired compared to the days of old. I find the large doors in the entryway to be of interest, but the rest of the place is lost on me as I find myself immersed in a sea of camera-wielding tourists shuffling through the stone arches like overfed sheep.

Heading back to the hotel we stop at a huge bookstore called The Book Shed. Chris feels it would be respectful to the English to buy a book by Clive James. I wander around and end up picking a book by John Grisham. I am not proud of my choice, but I need something for the train ride tomorrow that I can read without having to concentrate.

The only book I brought on the trip is Don Quixote. I have always meant to read it and I figured this was the perfect time. I know it is an amazing tale, but I cannot talk myself into pulling it out and reading it for the life of me. Perhaps I will start it on one of our long train rides. We grab some ham and butter sandwiches on the way to the hotel.

It must be the excitement of the room, of having our own bathroom or the fact that we are leaving London tomorrow, but we're finding ourselves to restless to even consider sleeping. We head out to find something to drink and end up at an Italian chain of restaurants called Bella Pasta. The atmosphere is perfect and the coffee is superb. Across the street is a Taco Bell, and I am overcome with the curiosity of what a Taco Bell burrito will taste like in England. Is it boiled? Do they use lamb instead of beef? Clotted cream instead of salsa? I have to know so I purchase a burrito. Despite all the opposition this could cause back home, this is the best damn Taco Bell burrito I have ever had. Viva la England!

I don't think Chris is very proud of the fact that I have now eaten in two American fast food joints and we have only been here two days. I start to feel ashamed, but then remember that England is not known for its amazing culinary treats, and promise myself that this will not happen once we hit the mainland. We head back to the hotel and prepare for sleep.

I have brought with me a pair of thongs, or flip-flops, that I plan on wearing whenever we have to do the communal shower thing. The last thing I want to contract is some annoying fungus on my feet from some French Canadian biker club. In lieu of slippers, I put these on to visit the restroom and Chris cannot help but poke fun at me. I may seem strong on the exterior, but inside I am small and weepy. I suggest a particular area on his person for him to place his head and turn out the lights. From the darkness, he calls my name. "What?" I grunt. "Gee!" He says, "I wish I could borrow your thongs!"

This sends us over the edge. The mixture of a hard day, a strange bed, Taco Bell food and the fact that he is an asshole all turn this into the funniest thing I think I have ever heard. Ten minutes later we are in tears, laughing like idiots. The people next door bang on the wall for us to shut up. This, of course, sends us into worse fits of laughter for another ten minutes. We finally quiet down and drift off to sleep. Tomorrow we head North, to Nottingham, to visit my friend Nicole.

Waking up in our own room is a wonderful thing. The drawback is that we have slept in, and even though we rush downstairs, we still miss the cheap breakfast by a good ten minutes. The lady behind the counter offers us a candy bar as condolences for being too lazy to cook one more egg. This only depresses us and we leave.

Chris drags me back to the Taco Bell. This is not because he wants to sample the Mexican/English treat, no matter how good I make it sound. He only wants a picture of himself in front of the Taco Bell sign. I wrestle on whether or not to start my day off with a burrito, but it's closed when we arrive and my decision is made for me. I take his picture then we search for a hole in the ground. We need to take the Underground from Earl's Court to St. Paul's, or at least that is what Chris says needs to happen, I have been lost since we left the hotel room.

St. Paul's cathedral is too impressive for such a small name. I am thinking maybe it should be called St. Bartholomew's or St. Rotisserie's or something really big and religious sounding. Of course, St. Peter's in Rome is huge and Peter is a pretty small name, so I guess it all makes sense somewhere. Walking toward the cathedral, Chris says that the Catholics really know how to put on a good show. Chris hardly ever says anything positive regarding religion, and I think this would be a good way for the Catholic Church to advertise for converts.

Catholicism: We really know how to put on a good show

The doors to the church are huge and I make Chris take my picture in front of them. It would take at least thirty of me, standing on each other's

26

shoulders, to be as big as these doors. Of course, thirty of me would never be able to stop complaining enough to accomplish such a task, so that analogy is somewhat pointless. We go inside and to my right is the biggest organ I have ever seen. The pipes go as high as the ceiling. "Gosh," I say. "I wish I had an organ that big."

I hear snickers from the people behind me. It was meant to be vulgar, but only for Chris's ears. Apparently, my voice carries a bit inside of holy temples. Of course, now that I have said something disrespectful in the house of God, I have most assuredly put my soul in some sort of peril. There is a mass starting and I decide I had better attend. Chris goes to the underground crypt to see if he can find T.E. Lawrence's grave.

It's a matinee mass and the crowd is small. The priest asks us to come to the front and sit in the seats where the choir usually sits, to be closer to him. He is a very kind old man and he talks about God and humanity and following our hearts when making life choices. He looks content and peaceful and I wonder if I will ever be that happy. Of course, he has had years to get to where he is, so I am thinking I still have some time to work on it. I am sure a comfy robe, like the one he is wearing, could help a bit too.

He has us come to the center of the floor and hold hands, and then we say the Lord's prayer together. At the end he stands there with his eyes closed and I wonder if he has fallen asleep. Eventually his face breaks into a beam and I wonder if God just told him a good knock-knock joke. He looks at me and then winks and I am sure he has read my mind. He dismisses the group and we are set free to wander the halls of St. Paul's.

I find Chris with a look of concern on his face. I assume he did not find Mr. Lawrence's grave, but he says that he did indeed find it. He says it isn't a genuine gravestone. It is a bust on a shelf with a big plaque beneath it that says Lawrence of Arabia. He wonders if it would be more profound if it said T.E. Lawrence and then maybe a quote or something. He says he is happy that he saw it, but it was a bit disappointing.

I run downstairs to see what he is talking about. It looks less like the guy in Lawrence of Arabia and more like my best friend from high school. I decide not to tell Chris that my mass experience was better than I had expected and that the priest can hear knock-knock jokes from above. I mumble something about the mass being pretty good and then we leave the church.

On the steps are droves of people milling about. Backpackers, tourists and kids playing hooky, all lounging in the brief strand of sun that has found its way through the clouds overhead. At the bottom of the stairs is a man selling ice cream cones. We partake and join the others in watching the world go by. I am trying to get some photos of a few of the people with the more interesting faces, but it's too hard to hold a camera and an ice-cream cone at the same time. The ice-cream cone prevails.

Eventually the sun abandons us and the clouds invite a cold wind to join them. The land of Tony Blair, Afternoon Tea and Shepherd's Pie has been good to us. We finish off our ice cream cones as we head for the train station.

CHAPTER THREE

Nottingham

Robin Hood, Demonic Possession and English Ale

We are on the train from London to Nottingham and the batteries in my Walkman have died. Chris is trying to write in his journal, but he is facing the back of the train and is informing me that he may be spewing Corn Flakes in about twenty-five minutes.

I am flirting with a three-year-old girl. Chris says that with her blond hair and ice blue eyes she looks like a little elfin-child. She and I are making faces at each other and waving our hands in the air. I am going cross-eyed and she is dutifully imitating me. I can tell we are starting to annoy those around us. Chris says she is on her way to visit her nana and papa, though how he came across this information I do not know. She sticks her tongue out and I roll my eyes in response.

We arrive in Nottingham and wander through town toward Trent University. This is where my friend Nicole is attending for a semester. I met Nicole at the University of Arizona a couple of years earlier. We were friends for a while, lost touch, and then one day I started getting postcards from

Europe. She had decided to take a semester overseas. She lives in a dormitory that is set aside for incoming freshmen and exchange students. Her floor has more nationalities represented than last years Olympics.

We will be staying in her friend Felicity's room. Felicity is from Australia and is going to be out of town for a few weeks. She left us a note on the bed that says,

Have fun, enjoy the view, drink leaps and do not fart in the bed.

I love the way Australians are straight to the point. I know I talk in my sleep, but I cannot truthfully say what other bodily functions I have control over, so I give Chris the bed and I take the floor.

After dumping our backpacks, we go to a pub with Nicole and a few of her friends. Gooseberry Pub is by far the most crowded place I have ever been. It is wall to wall people, and as I force my body through them to gain the bar, I feel like a sperm, fighting with millions of other sperm, trying to reach the egg. We eventually elbow our way to the counter and begin our quick journey into inebriation. I start with some Guinness, but am given shit about drinking an Irish beer while visiting England. I explain that I have no idea what any of the other stuff is and they take this as a sign to choose my drinks for me.

One of Nicole's friends returns with a pint of some sort of black liquid that has the consistency of motor oil. It is called Black Arrow Cider and I am only able to drink a third of it before it starts to make me nauseous. It is not so much the taste that I find dissatisfying as it is the need to chew my way through the thickness of this stuff. We decide to go to a club and do some dancing, but I have not finished my beer yet. Finding myself the victim of peer pressure, with all eyes upon me, I do the only thing I could at this point. I chug the rest of this black sludge and head for the door.

I almost make it to the exit before the effects of the Guinness and the WD40 hit me full force. Finding the doorway, I stumble ahead of the group and down a flight of stairs that have now become very difficult for me to navigate. There is nothing better than a lightweight American drinking European beer. Luckily it is cold outside and this brings about a bit of sobriety. We go to the dance club on campus called The Sub.

Normally I am not one to get on the dance floor without first being dragged and threatened, or at least beaten into submission, but with that pint of cider and the disco beat I am ready to shake my money-maker. We dance for at least three hours, and I cannot drink enough beer to keep me hydrated, much less drunk. Nicole has a few words with the DJ and then comes back with a smile on her face. Over the loudspeaker we hear, "This next one goes out to Vince and Chris of the U. S. of A."

For the next ten minutes, we are bopping to the extra-long dance-mix of YMCA. Chris says that he will never have to dance again after gyrating to what he considers the most important of dance tunes, Dancing Queen, YMCA and I Will Survive. We leave the club a little after one in the morning and head back to the dorms. Our group is a strange mix of intoxication and exhaustion and I have a feeling I am going to happily snore extra loud tonight.

After a bit of a sleep in, we wander around Nottingham. It is a quaint town with its brick streets, little houses and spattering of pubs. We wander over to Nottingham Castle, the setting for the famed story of Robin Hood. The whole of one side is covered with vines and the gardens surrounding the castle are magnificent and reminiscent of a rain forest. There are two kids in the front lawn sword fighting with wooden sticks. They are loud and unruly, and are managing to shatter the sereneness of the moment, but then one of them slips and falls in the mud with a big splash. This makes me smile.

We go to see the Robin Hood statue. He is regally pulling back his bow, arrow at the ready. At one point Robin's bronze bow and arrow were stolen by vandals and the new ones are made of steel. Fortunately, they look like they were made this way on purpose. We pose with the statue. Chris does a more natural pose with the statue gallantly poised behind him. I stand with the arrow pressing against my temple and a look of terror on my face. My attempt to have nice photographs for later knows no boundaries.

We stop by the market and pick up food for tomorrow's picnic and today's dinner. Back at the dorm we make a big bowl of spaghetti that half the floor samples. We have bought baguettes and I cannot stop myself from dipping them into the spaghetti sauce to see if it is done yet. By the time dinner is ready I have to force myself to eat another bite.

Later we tramp over to Trip to Jerusalem, which is believed to be the oldest pub in all of England. It is half built into a side of a hill and the whole interior looks like a cave. There is even a hole above the bar for the smoke to find its way out. The history is that this place was a stop off point for pilgrims' back in the days when pilgrimages were the hip thing to do. Chris says it looks like it would be a good setting for a movie, all cramped, smoky and filled with good cheer.

We are drinking something called Kimberly Classic, which does not taste all bad and is slowly doing its job on my ability to enunciate. We then head over to a theatre called the Odeon, to see The Exorcist. This is first time Chris has seen it and he says it is quite disturbing. Of course, he goes on to explain, possession by Satan usually is. I wish this had been my first time on the big screen instead of on a rinky-dink video. I appease myself with an overabundance of Gummy Bears and an ice cream sandwich. Chris is forcing down Gummy Bears, licorice and some kind of weird ice-cream cone shaped like a chicken drumstick.

Leaving the theatre, we are more than spooked. We decide to take a short cut through campus to get back to the dorm, and to cut down on the off chance of a possible demonic-possession. This short cut requires the crossing of a busy street near a blind bend in the road. This idea seems only slightly stupid as we run across the street between careening vehicles flying around the corner. Unknown to us, there is not only a cement divider in the middle of the road, but also a rod iron fence that comes as high as our waists.

Normally this would not be an obstacle, but it is dark, and running into it without knowing it is there, is not the most celebratory of occurrences. Luckily I am padded by the recent consumption of Gummy Bears and only suffer minor embarrassment. We scale the fence and make it across the other side of the road, only to find that a fog is starting to descend.

A fog is the last thing a people who have just watched demon possession should have to contend with. Luckily, our group has become loud and obnoxious and the only people wanting to kill us are the inhabitants of all the households within a quarter mile range.

As we get back to the dorm, Chris, Nicole, and a girl named Vicky decide we should discuss politics. It is an amusing conversation as Vicky talks about how much she likes Clinton from a European's standpoint and Chris and Nicole vehemently disagree. Fulfilling my role as devil's advocate, I can not help throwing in that at least he is not as bad as Reagan was.

This is the beginning of the fireworks as we discuss America, the world and all other matters pertaining to the issue of our political leaders. At one point I find myself making a point while talking with a thick English accent. Vicky and Nicole do not seem to notice, but I see Chris giving me a look that says, what the hell are you doing? I cannot explain this behavior and am wondering if this will someday get me beaten to a pulp in some middle-of-nowhere country pub. We finish arguing around two in the morning and head off to bed.

Lying on the floor, drifting off to sleep, I accidentally say to Chris, "You really do like Clinton don't you?" This starts him up again and we are yelling and calling each other bad words until four in the morning.

Five hours later our host awakens us. We debate on whether or not to go to Sherwood Forest and see the famed tree where Robin Hood and his men of merriment spent a lot of their free time when they were not robbing, pillaging and procreating. Nicole says that there is a bike tour we can take that lets us ride through the forest to the tree. She adds that the tree itself is not that big of a deal and there is nothing else out there for miles. " Plus," she says. "The forest is not really a forest anymore, as it has sort of shrunk a bit."

We decide instead to go on a picnic, which is fine with me, as I have no desire to sit on a bike and peddle my way into a barren clump of trees whose only claim to fame is historical housing.

We walk through town and begin to notice that something is amiss. There is an eerie silence around us and there is not a person in sight. No stores are open. I begin to fear that perhaps there has been some sort of biological accident that has caused the town's residence to flee in horror. We walk by a Burger King and its lights are off. In America, Burger King never shuts its doors. Now I am really frightened.

Nicole explains that these odd occurrences are due to what the Europeans refer to as *Sunday*. We laugh, but realize she is not kidding. I had heard about this back in America, things being closed on Sunday, but thought it was something that had slowly disappeared as Capitalism made its way into Europe back in the early 19th century. But here, things really are closed, shut, without a soul in sight. The odd thing is that there is not anyone that is opening their doors to take advantage of the fact that everyone else has closed theirs. Now THAT would be the true capitalistic way!

We see a pub full of patrons and find out that they are allowed to open for two hours during the day, to serve lunch, but not alcohol. Of course, if you can find a pub owner that would refuse you a pint to toast his health with, I will pull a rabbit out of my sleeve. Luckily the buses are running as we clamor aboard and head towards Wollaton Park. Toward the edge of town, out the bus window, I see a movie theatre and a Burger King that appear to be open. I ask Nicole about this and she sighs heavily. Apparently, not everyone can resist the tug of capitalism.

Wollaton Park is an early tower house that looks like a small castle. It sits high upon a hill that is surrounded by acres of green grass, forests and a couple of reed-lined ponds. Eight of us have gathered for this picnic and we are all equally struck with the beauty of the place. Cows and deer roam free in the fields and we try to get close enough to take a picture with them, while at the same time, avoiding a swift hoof kick to the head.

Chris is amazed at all the happy children and dogs roaming about. The dogs he especially finds amusing. He says that they actually seem genuinely happy to be bounding about in the grass fields. If I were a dog I would be chasing down a cow or one of the smaller deer, but bounding happily is also a good way to spend a day, or in their case, seven days.

It is too wet to sit on the grass so we picnic on a sidewalk. The five other people are friends of Nicole's that we have spent the last few days with. We find ourselves laughing and leaning against one another as if we have been friends forever. It's a strange feeling when you click with a group of people that you know have been by your side for who knows how many lives. After digesting our food we play some sort of keep away game with a tennis ball, at which I am fairly decent minus my uncanny ability to always step in mud. Or at least I hope its mud.

Chris has been able to procure some nice looking grass stains on his pants, but it was for the team and that is all that counts. I tell him that it seems so weird that we barely met these people and I like them like my best friends. He agrees, and adds that we will probably never see them again. My team beats Chris's six games to four. Afterwards we walk around the park, admiring the deer, as the day slowly becomes overcast.

This is to be our last day in Nottingham and the last day with our new friends. Sophie, the girl from France, says that she will be coming to America soon and perhaps she will run into me. I smile and decide not to tell her what a big place America is. Then again, this town of Nottingham has somehow brought this little group of people together. Maybe the world isn't such a big place after all. Next day, Chris and I are a bit sad as we board the train to Ossett

CHAPTER FOUR

York

Vikings, Fish and Chips and The Pet Shop Boys

I am lying in what is most likely one of the most comfortable beds in all of England. I was originally supposed to sleep in the loft, but when our host turned on the light, the first things I see are three huge spiders eyeing my head hungrily. She gave them a good smack with her slipper but I could not get out of my head that their immediate family would now want to extol revenge on the humans. Chris is now sleeping in the loft.

We arrived in a town called Wakefield and took a taxi to friends of Chris's parents, Mary and David. The taxi ride came out to four pounds ninety and Chris handed him six pounds. We left the cab, only to have him yelling at us that we had given him too much money. I guess the book was correct, one does not tip cabbies in England.

Mary had a traditional English meal of potpie and peas waiting for us. It was perfect gray weather food and I was happy as a clam. We then poked around the house for a bit, wrote in our journals and headed off to bed. A big comfy bed, which is now slowly sending me off to dream land.

It is too early in the morning but Chris says we need to get ready if we are going to make the bus to Wakefield. Mary walks us to the bus stop and flags down a bus for us. You can tell she is nervous about leaving us on our own and I can't help but think how much our mothers must be worrying about us back home. We called them when we landed in London and then told them we would not call again for at least a week. Of course, for all we know, they may have already changed their names and vanished.

From Wakefield, we hop on the train to York, arriving in the early hours of the morning. We immediately jump on a big, red, double-decker bus. The tour is interesting and because of a slight mist, we have the entire top section of the bus to ourselves. We see the ruins of St. Mary's and one of the largest medieval castles in the world.

Mary has made us sandwiches of ham and butter, which are unbelievably good, but leave me with the smell of ham and butter on my hands and face. We are growing tired of the bus and are thinking of hopping off soon when the driver tells us to pay attention as we come around this next turn. He says that if anyone is sitting on the top, he recommends that they stand up and look straight ahead. We obey, and coming around the corner, catch our breath in unison.

We are across the city and on a slight rise. Before us is the most amazing sight, York Minster in its full glory. The size of the church itself is hard to describe. You do not realize how big it is when you are in front of it or even when you go inside. However, when you see it in comparison to the city itself, it is incredible. Half of city of York is the cathedral. It is like looking at an ornately carved mountain. I am too stunned to even think about taking out my camera for a picture.

After walking around York Minster, we stumble around the streets of York. There is a homeless lady sitting on the edge of the sidewalk up ahead. She is holding her head in her hands and has a little sign propped up against her legs. She looks up and me and I am surprised to see she must be in her mid-twenties. Chris wanders ahead.

People are slowing down to read her sign and then resuming their walks. We pass her but something bugs me and I go back. Once in a while, it strikes me that these people are someone's daughter, mother or sister. I sit next to her and we talk for a little while. I know people say that the homeless are oftentimes alcoholics or drug addicts, but who could say I would not be too if in their shoes. If it is a means of escape from something worse, than that is their choice. Then again, she could be none of those things, just hungry and having a bit of bad luck. We talk as two strangers would, about the weather and where we are from, nothing too personal and nothing too intrusive. I do not have much money on me, but give her what I can and leave her be.

We come to the shopping district, which is made up of the buildings that lean so far into the road, their tops actually touch one another. Chris sees a sweater that he is thinking of buying, but instead we just stalk it from outside the shop window for a good twenty minutes.

There is a guy replicating Renoir's The Boating Party on the sidewalk with chalk. It actually looks like the real thing. Next to the picture is a sign that says this picture is not for sale. I really do not see how it could be, since it is drawn on the sidewalk. Next to me, I see the tourists in their plaid shorts, black socks and dangling cameras. I wonder how many people have attempted to buy the sidewalk from him. I am glad he is not crafty enough to actually sell it to them. It looks like it is going to start raining and I fear for the artist and the boating party.

We hike up to Clifford's Tower, a round structure on a hill, a place the Jews fled to in 1190 to escape being killed by the Christians. The plaque says that the Jews, after fleeing to this spot, ended up taking their own lives. From atop the hill I can see the whole of the land and think of the history of this structure. My concerns take on an air of insignificance.

We are debating whether or not to go into the Jorvik Viking Centre. It is supposed to be an interesting place but Mary told us she went once and it really smells in there. We are not sure if she means that it smells in a bad kind of way or in a Viking kind of way. Of course, it would not help much if she had said yes to either of these. We decide not to go and instead head for the crumbling wall that surrounds the city. Walking around a city wall is more fun than one might think. Not only are we able to avoid the traffic and pedestrians as we go from one side of town to the other, it also offers a great view into people's back yards. I never would have guessed at the popularity of those plastic Pink Flamingos.

After reading all the plaques we could find, explaining who lived here, died there and lost their head a time or two, we decide to call it a day. Our train will not be ready for a bit so we head out of the station to play. To our left is York Minster, towering over everything. Across the street is a huge billboard of an American basketball player wearing high-heeled shoes. To our right is a wooden cutout of a train conductor pointing the way to the station.

Chris wonders if we have enough time to go back into the church for a bit, but I talk him into getting pictures of us with the wooden train conductor and that pointing finger of his. I smile sheepishly as I touch the wooden gentlemen's finger with my own. As I take Chris's picture, he sticks the wooden train conductor's finger in his ear. This time I am a little jealous. His will be the better of the two photographs.

We are back at Mary's in late evening. Her son-in-law, Les, and his two boys are here to meet us. He is an old friend of Chris's parents and they discuss the family back home. I wander into the living room and join the two boys in a game of cards. I am beating the older one at this game, but the little guy is kicking both of our butts. Both kids have thick West Yorkshire accents and at one point, the younger one says something to me that sounds nothing like the English my ears are accustomed to. I say, "Excuse me?"

He is obviously embarrassed and apologizes that it is hard to understand him because his accent is so thick. At this point his father walks into the room. He tells him never to apologize for his accent. He says it's a good strong one and he should be proud. I am beginning to like this guy.

Les finds me intriguing as we talk about my background, my beliefs and the fact that I actually voted for Clinton. He says that he has always thought he liked him, but was unable to really form an opinion just on what the English newspapers say. I tell him the good and bad points of his presidency and Chris sits to the side rolling his eyes in true Republican fashion. I have never really cared about Clinton or politics much, but having something that irritates Chris so easily is hard to nullify.

After a bit, Les crams us into his red sports car and takes us for a spin. He drives like we are being chased, which is even more frightening when you are not used to being on the wrong side of the road. I keep reminding myself that unless we meet up with a group of Americans, failing to drive in the correct English fashion, a car will most likely not come around the corner and hit us head-on.

He takes us to a pub called Carpenter's, for a pint. Here we meet up with Mary's brother Brian. Brian turns out to be another member of the fan club for Chris's father. Tales of his dad's old days are passed around and the beer flows freely. Brian asks me what my favorite musical group is, which is odd coming from a man who is most likely in his early sixties. I tell him that Erasure is my all time favorite and he laughs and says they are his too. Les loves The Pet Shop Boys, which thrills Chris to no end.

Talking to Brian is like talking to a person my age. It excites me to know that there is a good chance I can still be hip as I progress in years. We talk about America a bit. They make it clear that even though they tend to envy the speed and technology we appear to have, they kind of pity us for the lack of culture and history that we have to endure. Come to think of it, I kind of pity us too. We all agree that England has most of the world's best musicians and some of its worst food. Except for the seafood and potato concoction, which Les tells us we will love, as he has appointed himself the ambassador of introducing us to our first taste of world famous Yorkshire fish and chips.

As we walk out of the pub, the barkeep and a few of the regulars shout out, *Cheers!* This makes it the most perfect pub experience I could have ever wanted. Brian asks us where we are headed off to tomorrow and I tell him Inverness. He gets a faraway look in his eye. I ask him if he has ever been there. "No lad." He says, "But I mean to before I pass on."

At sixty thousand miles an hour, on what this country considers the correct side of the road, we get to the fish and chip place within no time. Les says he just wants to make sure they didn't close before we got here, but I have a feeling he would have driven this fast anyway. He jumps out of the car, gets the food from what looks like a small trailer on the side of the road, and hops back in. I have to hold this bundle of goods all the way to his house and the smell is making me ravenous.

His two boys are home, as is his wife, Susan. We talk into the night about our countries, technology and whatever else we could think of. It is interesting to be able to talk to someone from a different country, yet still speak the same language. It helps to feed the curiosity. The smallest of the boys tells his mom that he wants his hair like mine. By this point, it is long enough to put into a little ponytail and I apologize to her for the future argument this will most likely bring about. The fish and chips are as wonderful as Les said they would be and our last night in England is spent with a nice family and full stomachs.

CHAPTER FIVE

Scotland

Jack the Ripper, Eva Braun and Frightened Sheep

We catch the train in York to go up to Inverness. We have a seven hour train ride ahead of us and I can't wait to get a good look at the English and Scottish countryside. Though I now have batteries for my Walkman, somewhere along the way I seem to have lost a few of my cassette tapes. The only ones I have left are the Counting Crows and Enigma. I suppose these will have to do.

We are on the train early, so of course, I feel like crap. For some reason I keep forgetting to drink coffee, which means I cannot seem to break out of this morning haze, unless it is time to enjoy one of my lack-of-caffeine headaches. The country directly outside of York is not as inspiring as I had hoped and I slip off into a nice nap.

Waking, I find that we are in Northern England, and it is the England that I thought one could only find on postcards. There are farms, hedges and a wonderful beauty around us. The train is shooting across the landscape and yet the picture outside the window seems to be standing still. It is all very inspiring as I nod off again, but this time with a stupid grin on my face.

Chris is writing postcards and I think it's the scratching of his pen on the paper that wakes me. We are just crossing the border into Scotland and there is a definite change in the scenery. Outside our window is the brightest, most lush, green grass that I have ever seen. It is like no color green I could even imagine. Off in the distance are mountains, which appear like nothing more than shadows through the light morning fog.

I take out my journal to try and sketch what I can of this landscape. I am thinking that someday I will paint it and then be able to show others what I see. Deep down I know this will never be possible. I will never be able to produce something this beautiful on canvas.

There is a raging river zigzagging next to the train. It must be a good twenty feet across and it looks like it is covered with small rapids at every bend. The mountains have moved in closer and their blackness is in direct contrast to the bright green of the pastures. The grass is divided into sections with flat stone walls, crumbling at the perfect spots, but still doing their jobs with the small herds of sheep scattered around the landscape.

With the mist, the walls, the farmhouses and the sheep, I realize this is the Scotland that I have always dreamed of. I put on my Walkman and watch a whole other life unfold in front of my eyes. This is one of those times when I see a place that I know I belong, a place I know I have always belonged. At one point, Chris tries to get my attention but I pretend I do not notice. It is not that I do not want to talk to him. I just do not want him to ask me why my eyes are watery.

We arrive in Inverness toward evening and it is cold as hell. The only jacket I brought is a denim jacket and I am finding out that denim is not very good as far as warmth is concerned. We trudge through town but I am unable to shake the chill I have acquired. My teeth are chattering and my stomach is starting to cramp from shaking so much. I normally do not get cold, but when I do, my body definitely blows it way out of proportion.

I make Chris stop at an Italian restaurant and we go inside for some coffee. Two cups later and I am feeling better all around. Now, all we have to do is walk through town and up the hill to the hostel. Of course, going to the bathroom does not enter my mind until we are at least two blocks from the restaurant. I will admit, sometimes I even annoy myself.

Almost to the top of the hill and the clouds decide to let loose on us. It turns out to be more of a downpour than a rain and we are soaked rather quickly. The hostel has come into view and we are both dreaming of warm socks and crappy food and an evening of scribbling in our journals.

The great-granddaughter of Eva Braun is running the hostel. Ok, maybe she is not really her relation, but if there is ever a pageant to fill the position, she will definitely place rather highly. The price of the hostel is ridiculous and we can't help wonder if this is due to the fact that this is the only one in town. However, when homelessness is the only other choice, we tend to give in rather easily.

We are about to pull out our wads of Scottish money when she tells us that we are required to leave our shoes in the lobby. We look toward the lobby and see piles of shoes strewn about the floor. She explains that this is to keep the floors from getting muddy. Chris and I look at each other and without a word between us, re-shoulder our backpacks and head out the door. The last thing we want is to wake up and find out that someone has walked off with our boots. No thank you.

We stand outside in the rain for a bit and something up and across the street catches our eye. It looks like a small house hanging half over the mountain, but on closer inspection we see that it is a backpacker's hotel. We cross our fingers that they will have a room and we find we are able to get two beds for a huge chunk less then it would have cost us to stay in the house of Braun. Our beds have the distinction of being named after the Latin names of insects. The clerk's handwriting is hardly legible, but it looks like my bed is called Laphroaig. I will be sleeping on what I can only imagine is a centipede or something else with too many legs.

The hotel is a cute little number, consisting of three living rooms and a small kitchen upstairs, dorms and bathrooms downstairs. The kitchen is available to cook your own food, and there is an urn of coffee and one of hot chocolate for the guests enjoyment, provided you clean your cup afterward.

We are excited to throw our backpacks off and head upstairs to write postcards. Chris tells me that he has nothing against buying the postcards or writing the postcards, but sending them off is a big pain in the butt. Finding a post office is no easy task, and finding one that is open is even harder. My fear concerns the glue that is used on stamps in other countries. I sometimes wonder if their are strict guidelines as to where they get the glue that I so gleefully lick, or are they just grinding up every horse that falls over?

We are wondering where to eat and Chris says a pub would be nice. We are going to wait a while because it is still raining. Chris thinks this makes the city look nice. Realizing he has said the word nice in two sentences he wonders what is wrong with him. He thinks that maybe he needs Verbal Advantage. I think he needs to get Hooked on Phonics.

The rain finally stops. We begin our quest for nourishment. We cannot locate a pub to save our lives and without the obnoxious neon lights that point the way to food, like in America, we are clueless where to eat in this city of wet, stone buildings. We end up at a Pizzaland Express, which has an amazing deal, all you can eat for £2.99. We are too excited for words and proceed to stuff ourselves silly. Warm grog from a pub would have been nice, but you can still see smiles on our faces as we work in yet another slice of pizza.

We waddle back to the hostel and sit in the living room to drink tea. The room sleeps six and we are in no hurry to meet the people we will snore next to and then never see again. Chris is a little nervous about sleeping with strangers only because he doesn't know who is and who is not a psychopath. I suppose having your neck exposed for such a long period of time can become a little nerve racking. He chooses to sleep on the top bunk and I wonder if that is because he is hoping a psychopath will be too lazy to climb.

I do not like sleeping with strangers because I do not think my habits of talking in my sleep and loud snoring are very nice things to do to people I have just met. The trick I have learned is to lay on my stomach and then tuck the sheet in so tight I cannot turn over. This keeps me from snoring and also allows me to feel like a giant burrito. I am hoping that someone else will begin to snore so loud that my additional musical accompaniment will go unnoticed. I go to bed late and everyone else is sleeping. No one is snoring. Damn!

The next morning I take a shower with two women. It's not as great as it sounds. The showers are communal, which means everyone that has to use them, does. At first I freak out when I think I have walked in to the women's shower, but the girl wrapped in the towel tells me to come inside and that they are for everyone. If there is a cool bone in my body I will strike up a conversation with the unclothed girl in the little stall next to me, but it is too early in the morning to think about having conversations with a naked woman, so I let the moment slip by.

Chris does not like this arrangement. He says that communal showers work better in theory than in practice, making the point of how often do Cindy Crawford and Elle Macpherson stay in a hostel? I know when I cannot win an argument. I do however think that showering with a roomful of women beats showering with a roomful of guys any day, but that's just me.

I go upstairs to wait for Chris. The big window in the sitting area overlooks both the River Ness and St. Andrew's Cathedral across the way. The image is wonderful and I immediately sit on the couch and start to sketch it in my journal. On a chair in front of the window is an attractive Japanese girl drawing the same scene. She sees me sketching and comes to sit next to me. She watches me sketch for a bit and I watch her. My drawing is so rough compared to hers, but she seems to like what I have done. We exchange drawings, nod our approval and then hand them back. She knows no English and I can barely find Japan on a map. Luckily, neither of us wants to get tangled up in languages, so we just smile at each other and continue drawing.

When Chris comes up I clean my cup and am ready to go. As we walk out of the room the Japanese girl smiles at me and waves. I don't think Chris notices this, nor does he notice that I have grown six inches taller.

We spend the day wandering around the city of Inverness. Last night I was wondering if the people here are aware of how magnificent their city is. Are there Inverness youth that can think of nothing better than to get away from this place? I am sure there are some, but I find it hard to believe that everyone is restless in a place so rich with history and grandeur. Or maybe that is just an American thing, to always want to uproot oneself and start again in a place no one knows you. I think I know the answers to my questions, but walking beside a river and looking at castles under cloud-filled skies, I like to imagine that if I grew up here I would never want to leave this place.

We wander up to Castle Hill, and the regal Inverness castle. It looks wonderful from afar, but up close it has curtains on the windows and Hondas parked out front. It is now used as part of the courts and Chris says the only way we are going to get inside is if we are found guilty of something. We wander across the river and look around St. Andrew's. It is one of the more impressive churches we have seen so far.

We walk along the River Ness and I spend half my time trying to get a picture of the old clock tower on the other side, minus all the stores and cars. It is weird to see so much modern day items mixed in with historical things, but unless you close off the town as a tourist attraction, the people here need to function as a modern day society. It is damn cold here and a newspaper confirms that this is Scotland's coldest April on record. The chill I got yesterday was not from the temperature, but from a wind chill that was almost below freezing.

We walk to the middle of a bridge and Chris decides to throw a coin into the black water. We are stunned to see it hit the water and then float all the way to the bottom. What we think is black water is actually the bottom of the river showing through. I do not think I have ever seen water this clean and clear before. It seems almost unnatural. Sometimes I just hate where I come from.

We walk down to the shopping district and find a spattering of little stores open for our amusement. We go in one that sells Scottish goods. It is obviously for the tourist trade, but we are drawn to shiny things. Chris is considering the purchase of a kilt or perhaps a bagpipe. I can't decide if I should annoy the lady by asking her to trace my Scottish roots, which would be more than impossible to find. I am a little ticked that my family doesn't have a crest or a seal or even a little swatch of flannel to call our own, but I suppose that is just the price I will have to pay for not being a Scot.

We head down the street and decide that we need a good fish and chip meal. It is still a little early in the day, but that does not deter us from daydreaming about vinegar-soaked sea creature. I ask an older gentleman where the closest fish and chips would be. He points up the street and says, "Just up there a wee bit."

I am jumping for joy as I try to explain to Chris how perfectly Scottish it is. The word 'wee' can make me do cartwheels. We walk up the road and another gentleman crosses our path. I ask him the same question and he gives me the same answer. I grin so big my cheeks hurt. Chris tells me to knock it off, but I do not let him bring me down. Not a wee bit.

The fish and chip guy is barely opening when we arrive. We tell him we will hang out while he gets ready. We sit on the stone benches in the middle of the shopping area and I notice some graffiti that is a heart with the words Sharon-4-Brian in the middle. For a full minute, I cannot figure out what '4' means. Eventually I get it and am thinking that going this long without coffee may not be good for my health after all. I take a photograph of this Scottish hieroglyphic and cannot wait to show others back home.

The fish and chip guy calls us over and gives us some newspaper wrapped food. He talks to us for a bit and it is obvious he is not Scottish. We can not quite place his accent, but he is a very nice fellow and he completely squashes any fears I tend to have about undercooked fish. After walking the town for a while longer, we head to the train station. We are on our way to Edinburgh.

The trip to Edinburgh is through countryside that defies description. Chris is amused at the way the sheep run from the train in fear. We keep seeing people on the side of the tracks stopping to wave at the train. After a bit I realize maybe they are not actually waving at the train, but to those of us inside of it. I feel guilty and wonder if they all think I am a snob. I begin to wave over-enthusiastically at those we pass, thinking that perhaps they will spread the good news at their next village festival.

I have decided that I could work as a train conductor, but only if I could do my conducting here in the Scottish countryside. I have been listening to Enigma's Return to Innocence. Hopefully the title will prove itself to be ironically appropriate by the time our trip ends.

Chris is scribbling in his journal. Earlier he was saying that my journal is being written as a record of the deep thoughts I am having. He claims to be covering the more mundane aspects of life and this trip. I don't know whether or not to take offense at this, so I do. I tell him that I never think I do much writing. I feel that I just sort of doodle with letters. He likes this so much he quotes me in his journal.

Upon our arrival in Edinburgh we decide to find the hostel before it gets dark. At first we are thinking about staying at a backpacker's hotel that is famous for something or another. The name of it is Bob's or Rick's or some other one-syllable name, but then we begin to hear rumors that it is a cheap, unkempt place that rents you a mattress to collapse on after you come crashing down from your drug-induced high. We do not know how much of this is true, but this sounds like another place that we might run the risk of losing our shoes, so we decide against it.

We instead go to the High Street Hostel. Three other guys, who have obviously been here since the end of the Carter Administration, occupy the dorm room we are given. They have staked out their territory with every item imaginable and have made the areas around their bunks to look like home. We can only assume their homes look like shit.

Chris says that they have established their domain with their scents and assumes by the amount of pictures they have tacked to the walls, that they have either been here for more than a few days or they are all suffering from some major separation anxiety. They seem nice enough and even though I chain my backpack to my bunk with a heavy-duty bike chain, I assume that leaving town quickly would be near impossible for them to accomplish with all the packing they would have to do. We decide not to acquaint ourselves with our bunkmates and instead go out to have a look around. We are wondering if anyone will have the initiative to open a window while we are gone.

The rain subsides and the clouds part just enough to let in a shaft of orange sunlight. Its reflection off the stone walls is almost too bright to bear. Edinburgh becomes a shimmering painting of grays and browns and it probably looks exactly the way it has for centuries. As dusk nears a cool wind begins to blow. We are across the main bridge that connects the two sides of town. From this location, in the day's fading light, we see an influential sign. It is the red glow of a Pizzaland Express, and from here, hunger guides our feet.

While eating our dinner-without-end, or buffet as they call it, another

American approaches us. His name is Larry and he says he has not seen anyone from America for quite a while now. We talk to him for a bit and discover that he is from West Virginia and has been traveling around Europe for over two months now. He says that he just moves from place to place and works odd jobs whenever he can find them. He has a big mass of shaggy hair on his head. I think he looks like Richard Marx and Chris says he looks like a Michael Landon. He is wearing a Metallica T-shirt, but informs us that he also likes AC/DC quite a bit. We decide not to tell him who his hair reminds us of.

He asks if we want to meet up later to wander around town and we decide we will. It is exciting to be with someone who knows the places that are strange to us. I think of our roommates, and not having to spend a single minute more with them than I have to, and this makes it all the more sweet.

We hook up with Larry after making sure our bags have not been lost, eaten or smoked. He asks us if we have ever gotten lost in a city and I cannot think of a time that I have not been lost in a city. He says we will play a game that he loves. We will take turns picking the direction we walk until we have become completely turned around. The first time he says go left, I am turned around enough to not be able to tell which way North is, but it's fun to pretend this is not commonplace for me. We turn left again and then take two rights. The good thing about being lost is that it doesn't matter which road you take. We turn left again.

It takes a bit for Larry and Chris to become disoriented, but we eventually walk up to what looks like a university campus and they both admit that they have no idea where we are. The sun has abandoned us and Edinburgh at night is spooky. There is a row of hedges that head into a dark, wooded area and we start to walk in that direction.

Suddenly, a shape detaches itself from a tree and staggers toward us. I almost scream. We back away from this drunken madman. He garbles something with his over-intoxicated lips and then begins to run toward us. We turn and run, and though he is not going fast enough to catch us, he does not give up the chase for a good block or two. We laugh our nervous laughs and continue on our way, occasionally looking behind us to see if the drunken lunatic is persistent in his desire to dismember us.

We come across a store that seems to specialize in the sale of candy, ice cream and cigarettes. The store is actually a hallway with a counter and I find it hard to navigate with two other guys while trying to avoid knocking over the bubble gum racks. We are trying to decide what we want and eventually ask for some ice cream cones. There is nothing like a scoop of cold ice cream after being chased by Edinburgh's version of Jack the Ripper. The balding, older gentleman serving our ice cream notices our lack of Scottish accents and asks where we are from. I tell him Arizona and he says, "Tucson?"

This of course renders us speechless as we wonder how this guy knows about Tucson. We tell him Tucson is where we went to university and he explains to us that his brother lives there. He tries to visit him at least once a year. It's weird to know that even though you find yourself somewhere completely foreign, a place you never thought you would be, there is always someone there who shows you how small the world really is. I almost want to play the six-degree game with the guy, to see if we know his brother, but we may figure out that he and I are siblings and this would be just too much for me to bear right now.

We discuss the Arizona heat, which is the main topic of conversation whenever Arizona is involved, and bid him a fond farewell. Chris and I discuss coming back to his store before we leave Edinburgh, but by the time we have walked half a block, I am lost again.

Larry figures out where we are and he wants to check out a club, called the Beehive, that he heard is pretty cool. The Beehive is packed to the rafters, but we manage to wedge our bodies in far enough to buy a beer and mingle with the locals. The band is really good. They play a mix of Blues, Jimi Hendrix and U2. The smoke, the tight bodies, and the over-extended guitar riffs eventually get to us. Chris decides to wait outside. I ask Larry if he plans on staying longer and he informs me this is one of the coolest places he has ever been. I take this as a yes and tell him we will see him later.

Sitting outside the club, we cannot decide whether or not to go back to the hostel. We are both tired enough to go to sleep, but we feel like losers leaving such a hip place because of it being too loud and too crowded. We stand around outside and listen to the people having fun, but this makes us feel even more like losers and we eventually find our way back to the hostel.

Luckily, we discover that the reason our roommates were home during the day is because they stay out all night. We both smile as we prop open the window and crawl into our beds to sleep the sleep of the Scots. I even let myself fall asleep on my back, ensuring I will snore. I figure it is the least I can do, should our bath-challenged roommates come home.

By morning, our roommates still have not returned. Chris takes his communal shower first and comes back with a story. He says that a girl bumped into him in the bathroom, and when she said sorry, her voice was deeper than his. Of course, this intrigues me, but the only people that sound like men during my shower actually look like men too. We leave the window open for our roommates to enjoy. The room has already taken on a nicer, spring like air to it. A small gift from the Americans.

We spend the day touring the city. We walk the Royal Mile, which consists of the Holyrood Palace, Moubray House, St. Gile's Cathedral and the Parliament House. At the end is the Scotch Whisky Centre, what we call Whiskey Row, which is only amusing if you have ever been to Prescott. We head up to Edinburgh Castle, which sits majestically on the side of the hill, overlooking the city. We wander up to the entrance and ready ourselves for a cheesy tour of some sort, but the gates are open and we saunter in like hooligans.

The part that intrigues us most is the dungeon, which is not only in good working order, but is also accessible to those of us who want to climb into a cell and pretend that we have been naughty. Chris closes the door on me and then is unable to open it again. I think he is joking, but a good shove from my end does no good. I am wondering if he will leave me to die or use this opportunity to blackmail me. If the tables were turned, I would be trying to extort all I could from him, so I am not feeling very comfortable with my immediate future. After some banging, shoving, heaving and weeping on my part, the door finally swings open. I have survived my first prison-like ordeal.

I have heard a rumor once that somewhere in the castle is supposed to be a Medieval, scientific device that projects a 360° reflection of the city into a large bowl. I suppose it is a way to watch approaching armies without getting your head shot off. Then again, if they are close enough to shoot off your head, looking at them through a dish does not seem like the best thing to be doing.

My curiosity and lack of knowledge are not appeased on this issue because the large bowl device is off-limits today. We go look at the giant cannon, Mons Meg. Did I say giant? This thing is more than just giant. It is absolutely enormous! This cannon is the one you would use should you ever want to use an elephant as a projectile. They do not have anything to show the size of the cannonball that actually shot from this massive weapon, but I would assume that if they ever needed to fire it nowadays, a Volkswagen bug would do just fine. The plaque says that this cannon was made in 1449 and is still fired during certain city celebrations. I wonder how many people lose their lives, or ability to hear, during these jubilant occasions.

We go to the war memorial and find we are the only ones within. It is a massive building, and along the walls are the names of Scotsmen and women who have given their lives defending their country. Off to the side is a smaller chamber containing a book of some importance resting upon a pedestal. We are not able to get close enough to see what it is, but the room itself is so ornately, yet respectfully decorated, even a pub's menu would seem magnificent.

We wander the cobblestone streets of the castle and to the argyle battery to take some pictures near the smaller cannons that still point off the castle walls. I try to straddle one for a photograph, but they are quite wide and I am putting my groin in great danger, so I settle for a stupid picture of me just standing near one like a goof. We find the Scottish Royal Crown Jewels. We do not actually find them, they were never lost, but we do wander in to the place they are kept. They are very impressive and look like they could bring in a pretty penny at a pawnshop. On the way out, we notice a guard outside of the gates.

I am debating on whether or not to get a picture with him, both because he is carrying a rifle and because he is wearing a kilt. I cannot decide soon enough and he marches back into the castle. Then I notice a small wooden building off to the side. It looks like an outhouse without a door and inside is a life-size, wooden carving of a guard that looks so real it is creepy. We are excited to get our pictures with this over-sized Pinocchio and we find that if we take the picture far enough away, it does look like a real guard.

Chris goes first and crawls into the little wooden shed that houses the wooden man. The picture is of Chris with his chin resting on the guard's shoulder. It is beyond wonderful. It is my turn and to my chagrin, I discover that I am just too fat to fit into the little shed surrounding the guard. Of course, we could move the guard out of his little home, but this would defeat the purpose of the whole thing. Instead, I just take a stupid picture of me in front of the guard that looks like I am asking for directions. If I knew this was going to happen, I would have planned on losing weight before this trip.

We then wander up Calton Hill. Actually Chris wanders up to Calton Hill, I am just following him aimlessly and being amazed at all the cool stuff we are happening upon. I try to explain to Chris the beauty of not planning anything we do, but he has too hard of a time leaving things to chance. I tell him that he needs to let things work out and let other things not work out. Go with the flow, be like dust in the wind, and whatever other stupid thing I could think of.

My preaching is annoying him as I try to get him to see it all as just part of a life experience. He partially agrees with me but asks how he is supposed to undo 23 years of the way he has been, just do it? He says that if the pirates had been like him, they would have just sailed around a lot, looking for a nice island to land. I am thinking that if the pirates had been like me, they would have gotten lost within the first half-hour and then starved to death three hundred yards from shore. I guess, in a way, we both have issues.

Calton Hill is by far the most amazing experience I have ever had. It is not the old Greek columns or the view of the city or even the apples we find in my backpack that makes it so incredible. It is one of these places that just make sense to me. It just plunks me right down where I am and reminds me both how minute I am in the entire universe and how precious I am at the same time. It is cloudy, but the sun is finding its way down to us. There is a slight breeze in the air.

The city lies to the west and in the foreground is Duncan's Monument, a round structure I assume was built for Duncan. In the background is the city of Edinburgh, the castle and the surrounding countryside. We stay up here for at least two hours and I imprint the scenery, the smell and the emotions into my head the entire time. This will be my place to go back in my mind whenever I need an escape from life, and if that does not explain what I am feeling up here, nothing will.

On the way down, we stop at a cemetery. It is small, but the number of headstones and crypts is overwhelming. We wander around and read inscriptions for a while. There is a huge monument with a statue of Abe Lincoln on top. It is in memory of Scottish-American soldiers.

As we near the train station I see a man in a park being attacked by pigeons. He is short with gray tufts of hair like a mad scientist. The birds are on his shoulders and arms and one just landed on his head. I cannot decide if I should attempt to rescue him or let him die in true Hitchcock fashion. Luckily, I see that he is smiling and causing his own troubles by feeding the birds with handfuls of bread. I decide he is a crazy, mad scientist after all.

Back in town, we go to the National Gallery of Scotland. The walls are blood red and the paintings are magnificent. I see Bellotto's View of the Ponte Delle Navi, Verona, and he quickly becomes one of my favorites. The picture they have is huge, at least ten feet across, and the detail is amazing. The Monet's and the Van Gogh's are worth the price of admission. Eventually they make us leave and we wander the streets for a while longer before heading to the train station. We have booked two seats on an overnight train to London.

CHAPTER SIX

The English Channel

Sir John Gielgud and the Stuffy French Water Hostess

The trip from Edinburgh to London is pure hell.

We don't leave the station until one in the morning and the car we are in happens to be occupied by a group of fifteen high school kids who are not old enough to realize it does not take much to make others snap. The lights go off, as if they are going to let us sleep, but then are replaced by this odd bluish-green glow. It is not bright enough to read by, but strong enough that everyone around you appears to be in the middle of a bad bout of seasickness. Chris thinks the light is put in here to purposefully make you feel ill. I start to wonder how truthful this may be.

The kids continue to get louder and louder and I begin to wonder if they are orphans and have never had parental guidance. Maybe they are a hard-of-hearing club on a field trip. I keep hoping they will eventually nod off to sleep, but I think the volume they are emitting is to ward off the drowsiness that their wee brains are starting to feel. The train cannot go fast enough, the light cannot be green enough, and the only thought I have that appeases me is that I am not in a country where livestock is allowed to roam free within public transportation. Then again, if livestock were to get too loud, you could always kill it.

Chris is able to sleep fitfully by using his window as a pillow and his chair as a bed. The only way I am able to slip into a light coma is by cranking my Walkman up as loud as it will go and then drifting off to the sound of the Counting Crows. Unfortunately, every forty-five minutes my tape reaches the end, shuts off and the sound of the adolescent monkeys snaps me awake.

We arrive in London at seven-thirty in the morning. It is a weekday, and the English are going to work. We are foolish enough to try and squeeze ourselves, with our backpacks, onto the subway. It takes us five tries before we find a train with enough room for us to fit into. I feel like I am in a Japanese movie I saw once where they have guys whose job it is to smash everyone into the subway cars to make sure the doors will shut. I am being assisted by a nice English gentleman who, making sure the doors will close, shoves my backpack-laden body into the people in front of me.

The stop we are meant to get off announces that there is a bomb threat and the train will be moving ahead to the next stop. I can't help but wonder why the train is still passing through a terminal that is supposedly seconds away from exploding, but the people around me seem more annoyed than scared and I assume all is going to be OK.

We eventually get to a train that is supposed to take us to Ramsgate. There we will cross the English Channel and hit the European Mainland. We are in a rail car with a group of guys that are hoping to one-day retire as complete idiots. They are talking, yelling, swearing, and just pretty much advertising why testosterone is not always a good thing. Luckily the trip is not too long and after what we have just endured on our previous train ride, a burping contest would not phase us (nor surprise us with this bunch).

We arrive in Ramsgate and try to figure out how to get to Oostend, Belgium without ending up in Sicily or Rhode Island. The train leaves us off at one end of town and we have to get to the other side where the boats are. One would think that all we should have to do is point ourselves in the direction of the water and then take steps, but for some reason, it becomes much harder than this. The streets are cute and the houses are adorable, but nothing seems to go in a straight line. Pretty soon we are both cranky and hot and the only thing keeping us from killing each other is the knowledge that the last one left alive will still be lost in this stupid town.

We stumble upon a small grocery store and I happily enter with thoughts of a nice lady making me a sandwich. Unfortunately, this shop only sells things for you to take home, not to eat here, and we are even more disappointed to find that they do not specialize in an overabundance of junk food. We buy some crappy candy bars and a couple of sodas and I grab some cheese and a loaf of sliced bread. The next ten minutes we spend wandering toward the sea, eating cheese and bread sandwiches, which are neither good nor moist. We finally reach the water and are excited to skip down the millions of steps leading to the sandy beach.

We find that the giant, cruise ship is not due to leave for a while yet and takes almost two hours to chug its way across the channel. Neither of us is in the mood to wait and we inquire about the sleek-looking jetfoils we see leaving port every twenty minutes. They only take an hour to get across the channel and they cost an extra £7, but we figure out that we saved £9 by taking the overnight train from Hades to Hell, so that is enough to convince us to go for it. The next one does not leave for another twenty minutes and I am feeling ill from the sandwiches that we ate, so I grab a sausage to appease my stomach.

Being inside the jetfoil is like getting on a Disney ride. The seats are all facing forward, we strap ourselves in and there is an air of excitement as everyone pictures us slicing through the water at top speeds. What they don't tell you is that in order for the jetfoil to work, it raises itself out of the water, thus forcing the windshield to face the blue-sky above. There is not a drop of water in sight. After the first two minutes Chris points out that if we had taken the big ship, we could have walked around the deck and smelled the salty air. I am just trying to figure out the fastest route to a water closet, should I choose to become seasick later.

As we blast across the water Chris realizes he is sweating. He knows this cannot be a good sign. He thinks he needs some air and is wondering why they cannot just open a window. A hundred-miles-an-hour and we cannot open a window? Sometimes I find his complaining to be just what I need to take my mind off other things. He thinks this jetfoil experience is surreal. He looks around us and announces he has two words for me: braces and nose-hair clippers. He is on a roll and I just sit back and enjoy it.

He wants to know if men really get to a point, that nose-hair becomes an accessory? He points out that in the row in front of us, and three seats over, is a man that looks like Ernest Borgnine, with a little bit of Nikita Khruschev mixed in. Chris wants to know why he is smiling so much. Is he that happy? Does he always look that way? Then he points out a woman to the right, across the aisle, her eyes are bugging out, and he thinks she looks like a Chihuahua.

I am trying not to laugh and hoping that those around us do not speak English. Luckily, everyone is concentrating on his or her menu. Then he points to the guy two seats over from me. He says this guy really worries him and not because he looks like Sir John Gielgud with a dash of that funny-looking guy with the bushy eyebrows in The Hudsucker Proxy. Sir John has been rocking back and forth and wiping his brow, and just before the trip started, Chris says that he watched him have a major bloody nose. He narrows it down to the fact that he either doesn't like sea travel or that he is dying of something and wants to fulfill this one wish before passing on. Or maybe he is just ill.

He looks like he is on the verge of blowing some chunks and Chris decides that he must be sick. For a moment he is happy because he is not the one sitting in front of Sir John, but then becomes agitated when he fears being called upon to perform an emergency procedure for a cardiac arrest. What exactly that procedure would be I do not know, but it has gotten Chris very upset. The lunch cart comes around and Chris cries out, "Egad!"

We watch as the Sir John orders a lunch, wipes his brow and then digs in. When he finishes his meal he resumes his rocking back and forth, but he looks a lot better. Chris thinks the lunch was actually a ticket to better health for him. Then the duty-free cart rolls around and Sir John buys three bottles of Harvey's Bristol Cream. Maybe he is not ill after all, Chris offers, just a little too friendly with the bottle.

The air conditioning finally kicks in and Chris becomes happy again. Now we are watching the jetfoil attendants as they make the rounds with lunch trays and duty-free alcohol. I cannot understand why they would serve lunch on a trip that does not even last an hour, but I guess there must be some plan behind it. Maybe the food is over-salted and this helps them to sell more booze. If this is the plan, it seems to be working.

The attendants are French and have the combined personality of a dog dish. During the take off phase, they went through the emergency procedures like they had somewhere else to be. The distribution of lunch brought them no closer to smiles and the handing out of duty-free bottles only seems to be annoying them. I am assuming they are not working off commission. The thing that did amuse us though was that they are the ones that threw off the ropes that tied the jetfoil to the dock. Chris thinks it is funny that they have to do this in skirts, I am surprised that these women do much of anything at all.

We finally arrive in Belgium. We have decided not to stay in Belgium because we do not want to have to exchange money just for one night and we want to be closer to Amsterdam in the morning. We are taking a train that is supposed to go to Utrecht, right outside of Amsterdam. Of course, this is all according to what Chris says, for all I know I could be in Saudi Arabia right now.

We are at another of the many stops this train is making and Chris has his biggest European experience yet. He sees a little old man standing at a train crossing, wearing brown pants and a red sweater over his shirt. Over the sweater, he is wearing a green sports coat that is buttoned and looks a little too small. He has a beret on over what is left of his gray hair and he looks like he can do with a shave. Hanging from his lip is a cigarette and he is standing in front of a green field and some cows. Chris says he probably plays chess in the park, boules on the weekend and argues with Pierre over a glass of Sherry. Every now and then Chris reminds me why I like him so much.

CHAPTER SEVEN
Holland

Van Gogh, a Nazi Rally and The Clapper

We screw up the trains somehow and have ended up at Den Haag. We decide this is not too far from Amsterdam and are afraid to go any further now that night is upon us. The map says that the hostels are outside of town and if my thumbnail is measuring correctly, it looks like it could be a nice little hike. According to Chris, it is 4km from the station.

Instead, we walk over the tracks and head toward town. I see a hotel not far from the station and wander in to see if they have any rooms for the night. I am transformed into another world of dark oak tables and deep red carpet, all sparingly lit by dim, uncovered light bulbs. The man at the counter is wearing a lime green suit that looks to be made of some very thick material. He has red hair and a scraggly red beard and families of wrinkles surround his sad eyes. I am standing in front of Vincent Van Gogh.

Apparently, Vincent Van Gogh does not take travelers checks, which is all we have at this point. This is because the only person left in the deserted train station was a man with a mop who did not look to be in the money-exchanging business. We ask Van Gogh what direction the hostel is and he tells us that not only is it very far, but that it is most likely full this late in the day. He is nice enough, but his lack of optimism is not helping us out one bit.

After a few minutes of Chris and I mumbling by the door, he announces that he will allow us to stay in his hotel and that he will take our travelers checks. The price of the room is twenty dollars apiece, which includes a breakfast in the morning. He asks us if we would like to pay a little extra to have a hard-boiled egg with our breakfast, and though it is mighty tempting, we refuse.

We go up a narrow, wooden staircase that does not contain one level stair upon it. The hallway is fascinating because the walls are covered with the same blood-red carpet as the floor. Every inch of the wall carpet is covered with paintings. Paintings of all different shapes and sizes, each with its own uniquely ornate, and rather over-sized, gold frame.

The room is a pleasant shade of dirty white with two cots and a sink. The closet looks dangerous and the floor is uneven. I am excited as I tell Chris how this place looks like a place that the real Van Gogh describes having stayed at one time, including the beds and the sink. Chris is not as enthused. He says that the place looks like it is decorated in the turn-of-the-century Shit period, quite common during the reign of King Jim Morrison.

It is too early to sleep and my uncanny sixth-sense ability tells me that Chris is less than happy in our evening's lodging. I open a window and we hear shouting and music and what sounds like your general tomfoolery. There must be some kind of carnival or something going, and we decide it would be a good idea to join in the fun.

We wander down the steps and tell Van Gogh we are heading out to see what all the noise is. He tells us it is part of the celebration for the Queens Birthday. I thought that was tomorrow and I thought it was in Amsterdam, but he tells us that it usually starts a day or two ahead of time and that every city in Holland will be celebrating. Perhaps ending up in Den Haag is not such a bad thing after all.

As we enter the center of town there are hundreds of people milling about. Everyone appears happy and drunk and though there is no actual place that they are gathering for any particular reason, the streets are jam-packed as we make our way to and fro. There is a park with a pond and along the water's edge is a row of carnival-type games. I see an opportunity to spend my money and the nice people are more than happy to help me accomplish this.

I find the game that lets you shoot out a red star with a machine gun, and that is exactly what I am able to do. Of course, having the job of ruining my good time, the man points out a wee, tiny, barely visible fleck of red that one of my pellets apparently missed. It is so small I cannot even discern if it is really a red mark or shadow caused by his thumb. With a smile, he gives me the better-luck-next-time look and wanders off to screw another willing idiot. I do however get to keep my little card with the bullet holes in it, and am excited at what a wonderful souvenir this item will make.

After a while we decide that without an overabundance of alcohol coursing through our veins, these people are becoming quite annoying. We look for something interesting to do, but coming up empty-handed, head back to the hotel. Tomorrow we have to catch the earliest train possible into Amsterdam, as the festivities will begin at first light, and we are in no mood to miss any of it.

We wake up to find that the communal shower does not actually work, but instead, we have a communal bathtub with a communal showerhead lying at the bottom. The only way I can figure out how to use this is to stand in the tub naked and hose myself off. This is not too bad, except for the fact that it is cold in here, the water is only slightly warm and the door does not lock. I feel like an idiot and this does not exactly put me in the best of moods.

We wander downstairs for breakfast and find waiting for us a roll, a slice of ham, some cheese and an apple. Actually, these items are sitting on a table and we assume this is someone's breakfast, but when we sit at an empty table Van Gogh comes out of the kitchen and shoos us over to the food. Did he know we were on our way down or are we the only people in the hotel? If the latter is true, I could have enjoyed my morning hose-off a bit more.

He asks us where we are going and we tell him Amsterdam. He says to be careful because it is a dangerous city. In fact, he says, everywhere is dangerous nowadays. When he was a young lad, he use to go with his friends to Greece, to sleep on the beach and just have a good time. You cannot do that kind of thing today, he warns us, and it is too dangerous to be able to sleep on a beach anymore. He wanders back into the kitchen and brings us each a boiled egg. We did not pay for it when we got the room, but he gives it just the same. I wonder if this is a sign that he likes us, or if talking to us has convinced him that Chris and I will probably not survive Amsterdam.

He is wearing his green suit and as we are getting ready to leave, he pulls out a matching green sun-hat. If only he knew how much he looks like the crazed man who painted with so much passion. Chris sees the look in my eye, and after we walk out, tells me it is too bad the old guy did not come over and kiss me on the cheek before we left. He says it would have been like Van Gogh coming from beyond. I think it would have been dreamy, in a non-homosexual kind of way.

When the train arrives to pick us up, we notice that people are practically falling out of the windows. If this were India, there would be groups of families sitting on top of the train. Of course, if this were India, we would most likely be waiting for the train while sharing our bench with a sacred bovine. We cram our backpacks and bodies into a compartment and I find that somehow, between breakfast and now, I have developed claustrophobia. I raise my head and gasp for what little air is being let through a slightly cracked window. I look like I am doing a bad impression of a guppy, but I do not care.

For some reason, we did not think that it would be a problem getting in to the city. I have read that the estimated amount of people who attended the celebration last year was close to three million. Did we assume they all lived in town? Did we think maybe we should call ahead to book a room? Well, not exactly. Sometimes it amazes me at how stupid two people can be.

We disembark in Amsterdam and find this exit from the train station is the best way to enter a city. The doors open up into an immense brick courtyard. To the left is a huge building. It looks like an Orthodox Church, standing watch over the canal. Ahead, a bridge is curving over the canal and then leading casually toward the shops and houses. The heart of the city is just up ahead.

From our vantage point, it looks like the three million people have already arrived, and we wonder where we will be staying tonight. To my right is a guy offering to sketch my head for some Dutch money and to my left is the largest gathering of Hippie men and women I have ever seen. They are picking through each other's dreadlocks and rearranging their multi-colored smocks and the one who appears to be the head of the group is actually laying on the sidewalk eating grapes. Across the canal is a man juggling sticks of fire. I wonder if I have enough film for this city.

We make our way to the hostel and act like we do not notice there are a million and a half people just outside the door. We act shocked that there is not a room available and ponder what to do next. He asks us if we have made any reservations and we nod our heads side to side, the international sign that we are idiots. He comes around the desk and heads out the door, motioning us to follow him. Is he headed to an alley to beat us up and steal our bags? Is he about to set the partying crowd loose on us for being so incompetent? Like infants, we follow.

He takes us to this weird little shop. At first, I am thinking it is some sort of travel agency due to the amount of postcards showing island destinations. Then again, a good number of postcards have pictures of S&M rituals or strange sexual positions, so I am not sure what it is they sell here. Chris says the postcards are very educational because he did not know you could pierce every part of the human anatomy.

The room is as big as a walk-in closet and consists of many phones against the wall. There are a fair amount of bongs for sale and our customer service representative is sitting on a tall stool. She is very skinny and is wearing a dark brown, skin-tight outfit, which shows off her attributes. I would find her attractive if her face did not have the look of someone who has been chain-smoking since the womb. She gives us a once over, and says to the man, "Ze kunnen een van myn kamers huren."

He tells us to follow her, and we are surprisingly able to keep up with this stick-woman, even with our fourteen hundred pound backpacks strapped to our persons. She takes us to an apartment that is next door to a police station. This in itself offers us some hope. We climb an amazing amount of stairs that are so narrow we literally have to put one foot in front of the other. The door opens to what could very well be the coolest apartment in all of Amsterdam.

The decorations are not much and the items strewn about lack a sense of taste. However, the wooden floors, large open space and the three giant windows that open into the street are more than enough to make us happy. She tells us we can stay for one night and that she wants us to pay her in advance. She charges us what the hostel is charging. In her broken English, she informs us that we are to sleep in the bedroom off to the side, as she will be renting the upstairs and downstairs to other travelers. We are happy to not only find a bed to sleep in, but to have such a cool place to hang out. She waltzes her skin-tight, brown-clad, chain-smoking body out of there and we are free to settle in.

Chris is not too happy that we have to share a bed. It is a big bed, but that does not make him any happier. I do not think I am that bad of a bed partner and this makes me feel unloved. He suggests that perhaps I would like to sleep out on the couch. I suggest he bite me. Plus, I am afraid that the skinny lady might come back, see me on the couch and make me do what some of those postcards were advertising.

We are excited to have a bathroom and take showers like real people. I have the great notion of washing my clothes in the tub and then hanging them out to dry. We make ourselves pretty and then head out on the town. The Queen is having a birthday party and we want to show her we care.

Our apartment is one block over from the Red-Light District. We did not know this until we found ourselves suddenly window shopping for vibrators and inflatable women. The stores look like regular stores, but when you get to the window displays, it is just a giant mound of devices, all with the same thing in mind, to make you say Oooohhh!

The next block over we notice a lot of people milling around and what looks like tourist groups stopping and staring. We are heading towards them when a man, who wants to know if I want to see two women make love to each other, approaches me. I think I say something like, huh? He points to a club with pictures of naked people painted on the side and asks if I would like to see people having sex. I tell him I really had not planned on it and he counters with the proposition of my wanting to possibly watch a woman have sex with a dog. Chris has gotten far enough ahead that I am able to pretend that I am interested and want to see if my friend will come. Without looking back I catch up to Chris and scurry ahead.

We reach the droves of tourists and realize we are in the heart of the famous Red-Light District. What this consists of is streets of windows, much like those cute boulevards one strolls to do one's holiday shopping, except the displays consist of women in lingerie or bikinis offering to fulfill your sexual urges. I find this fascinating as hell

We walk up and down the streets, not being able take in all that we are seeing. At one point I go the wrong direction and find where they keep the, shall we say, less desirables. Walking down a darkened alley, I realize it is a dead end. At the same time, I hear a woman's voice telling me to come visit her. What I see ahead is a toothless, aged face, reflected in a mirror that has been rigged above her window and angled toward the open end of the alley. I mumble a no thank you and back out of the alley. She shouts at me to come back and I walk a little faster. I know for a fact that her door is not locked and you never know if she was a sprinter in her earlier years.

We stay within the groups of tourists and this makes us feel safer. After a while Chris is tired of this but I am thinking this is probably better than a day spent at Mr. Hefner's mansion. We make a lucky turn and find ourselves in what I can only call the best of the best. The girls we are seeing are amazing, and its not just them, I can also appreciate the time they have spent putting together their window displays.

We pass a huge window that shows a living room decorated with old Victorian furniture. There is a woman on the phone, one reading on the couch and a third idly passing the time watching people walk by. All three are in classy lingerie. They are beautiful enough to be professional models and the entire scene looks like a photo shoot for another one of Victoria's dirtier little secrets.

On the next block, we see the women we have heard about, the college girls, who do this for the extra money. There is a group of men hooting and hollering in front of one of the windows and we see a girl in her mid-twenties, stunning to look at and gyrating to a dance beat. The girl next door, just as pretty, decides she cannot hold herself still any longer and walks over to join her friend, moving to the rhythm. They are both wearing bikinis, and after some more dancing, decide to engage in some erotic lesbian dance moves. The crowds of men cheer them on.

I hear a woman a few doors down explain to a prospective customer that it only costs thirty American dollars to spend some time with her. Both of us swear we have been to high school with some of these girls. I tell Chris I think it is time we left.

After we leave the district, we discuss what we think of it all. Chris finds it both fascinating and disgusting. He says it was kind of like walking down a street of art galleries, but with prostitutes instead of art. He says that they are just on display so that people can look at the wares, and he points out how interesting it is that the words ware and whore are similar looking.

I do not really mind the way Amsterdam has faced the issue of prostitution. There seems to be a system in place that works quite well, but on the other hand, the thought of someone renting herself out like farm equipment makes me sad sometimes. I decide that I do not really see anything wrong with it, and I would have to keep my wallet at home during my weaker moments, but if this is what they have chosen to do, then so be it.

I just feel bad for the poor slobs who have had crushes on these girls since high school. They have spent their lives pining over what became of little miss so and so, completely unaware that for thirty dollars they could be her vertically challenged dance partner. At least the girls here seem to be much cleaner and safer then what you get where this is illegal. I think there is really only one thing that bothers me about it. Love has become a commodity. Where is the romance in that?

Back in the middle of town, Chris notices tall Amazonian women everywhere. He wonders if they are genetically breeding them within the city. At that height, he says, even the ugly ones look pretty. I try to explain to him that the less attractive ones usually have some exotic European feature that makes them worth noticing. He is guessing that with this many beautiful women, they must all be psychotic. Sometimes, inside of pretending to have conversations, I think we should just hum to ourselves.

Wandering the streets, Chris is wondering why we keep hearing the song I Will Survive. I decide not to tell him that there are probably more openly gay bars in Amsterdam, than anywhere else in the world. I do not think he has a problem with that, but after our Amazon women talk, I would rather not have any more of our deep discussions this evening.

Despite popular belief, pot is not completely legal here. You can smoke it, but only in designated bars. The pot is not allowed to leave the premises and you usually have to go to some dank, underground room to toke up. What I am finding cool is the smoking man's lottery, which are large jars of water outside of the bars. They place a shot glass on the bottom, and if you make a coin float down into the shot glass, you get a free joint.

We decide not to smoke any pot while in Amsterdam, and though we have been approached three times, have fought the urge to buy crack-cocaine from drugged-out freaks with last years bed head. In Edinburgh, the guy Larry that we were hanging out with, told me that if we are approached and we say no thanks, or go away, this is supposedly a sign that we are somewhat interested. I suppose playing hard to get is a bargaining tool in the drug world.

He said that if you really do not want to buy, that you just completely ignore them and they will go away. I try both methods and he is right. I wonder how he knows this. He also said that there are a ton of undercover cops that try to get you to buy from them. I guess entrapment is not much of a thing here. Then again, when you cannot get people for prostitution or pot, you have got to have something to go after.

We are getting exhausted and decide to find our way back home. The partying is crazy and every street is jam-packed. We walk by one bar and they start to play the song YMCA. The entire place erupts and I run in to take part. Chris stays outside as I make my arms form letters for the next five minutes. While I am dancing, I notice a man sitting off to the side of me. He is wearing a black, leather biker outfit and looks just like the guy in the Village People, cheesy black mustache and everything.

Suddenly, his friend, a huge Hell's Angel looking guy with three days of stubble and a vest that does not quite cover his three hundred and fifty pound frame, sits beside him. They talk for a bit, watch the dancing and then the Village People guy grabs the Hell's Angels guys arm and starts to gnaw on it like there is no tomorrow. I cannot help but laugh. I think this moment needs to be on Holland's next tourist poster.

Amsterdam: So, what's eating you?

Farther down the road, we hear a song that we have heard over and over all day. It sounds like it is in Dutch and we think it sounds a little bit dorky. The people seem to love it. The entire bar starts to dance and then it spills out into the street. We are caught in a spontaneous eruption of twirling bodies. We cannot get away so we join in. Then someone throws his beer, then someone else. Pretty soon, there is an assortment of beverages being lobbed through the air. A cup of beer lands majestically on the head of a bald guy in front of Chris and he is drenched with the spray. Tired, happy and smelling like winos, we finally reach our apartment.

We have two new roommates. They are really nice guys from Sweden. We all sit on the window ledges watching the mayhem below us. They do not speak English and we do not speak Swedish, so we just watch the people below and share our universally understood chuckles with one another.

One woman walks by with the most cleavage any of us has ever seen. Chris is wondering if she has a permit for those things. A bit later an extremely drunken gentleman staggers below our window, stops, bends over and throws up all that he has eaten since Christmas. We are thankful that we are three stories up. We entertain ourselves by watching who walks over, around or through this disgusting mess. Chris says it reminds him of watching the marching band step over the horse droppings in a parade. I am thinking this is really disgusting, but like a car wreck, it is hard to look away.

We finally go to bed and I am awakened around four in the morning by a group of four who have paid to sleep on the couches. They bang, drop and chatter their way to bed and I have half a mind to tell them to shut up. The other thing that is pissing me off is that Chris is sleeping through it all. I am not sure which bugs me more and am trying to decide if I should yell at the new neighbors or make Chris enjoy them with me. Before I realize that yelling would actually take care of both ideas, I nod off to sleep.

The next morning we pack up and quietly make our way out of the apartment. The clothes that I have so smartly washed are still soaked after hanging for twenty-four hours. I bought thick cotton garments to be sure that I was wearing durable items, but this makes them almost impossible to air dry. We go to the overly skinny, chain-smoking woman and give her back her key. I find her lack of personality a refreshing way to start my day.

I am walking with my wet clothes draped over my backpack and both arms. We find a Laundromat and I head straight for the dryers. After stuffing in my wet clothes, I push the start button only to have a man from the back of the room start to yell at me in Dutch. After making it quite clear I have no idea what he is saying, he proceeds to tell me in English that I cannot just stick my clothes in a dryer, but that I have to wash them first.

I try to explain to him that I washed them last night, but he looks at me with eyes of skepticism. I want to ask him how smart I would be to stick clothes into a dryer that weren't wet, but he eventually just decides to drop the whole thing and walks away.

There is a girl doing her laundry and we both notice how attractive she is. Of course, you cannot flirt with people when you do not speak their language and especially not in a Laundromat this early in the morning. Then she asks me if I am using the other dryer and we realize she is American. Normal stud guys would say something cool like hey, are you an American? Or hey, so you are doing laundry right? But the fact that she speaks English only makes her beauty intimidating and we spend the rest of the time reading Dutch-language magazines.

We go to the Christian Youth Hostel. Their rates are amazingly low but they are very strict in their rules. No drugs, no prostitutes and you have to be in by midnight or they lock you out. These are all fine to me, but then they say we have to be out by seven in the morning and I am thinking they are just starting to push this whole Christian thing a bit far. We really do not have any other choice so we grab a couple of bunks.

After a healthy breakfast of rolls and cheese, we head out to the Reijkmuseum. On the way there we see before us the Heineken Brewery and we both drift away into daydreams of a tour and free tasting, but the brewery is closed for some reason and the next tour is the day after we are leaving. Instead, we buy our tickets and wander into the Reijkmuseum. The entranceway and first three hallways are full of people, Japanese people. It feels like we are in Disneyland. It is so crowded that we can not even get close enough to see the paintings. We walk around for maybe ten minutes without any luck.

We find a map and head toward the Impressionist paintings. At least they will have some good art in there. However, as luck would have it, the museum is remodeling this section and the entire area is closed off. I am pissed. We march to the entrance and I tell the woman that we cannot see any of the paintings, the museum is too crowded and half the paintings are off limits. She says the only part that is closed is the Impressionists and I tell her that I only came here to see the Van Goghs.

Oh, she says, then you probably want to go to the Van Gogh Museum. Van Gogh museum? I thought this was the Van Gogh museum. No, she says, the Van Gogh Museum is in a separate building, across the courtyard. She takes back our tickets and gives us Van Gogh tickets. These tickets are yellow and brown and have a little piece of one of his Sunflowers printed on them. I skip across the courtyard with Chris at my heels.

We somehow enter the museum through the wrong door and end up in the area that is full of Van Gogh's studies and his influences. I am expecting more and am feeling let down at what I see. The next flight up puts us in a hallway with his smaller works. They are all behind a glass case and it is amazing to see thirty of his works displayed before me at one time. Wandering further we come upon what is the main Van Gogh room. I nearly hyperventilate when I see what is in here.

There are not too many people and there is enough room to see each painting in its entire. Before me is the gardens he painted while living in the asylum, the portrait of Dr. Gachet, one of his Sunflowers, the painting of his chair, and to my shock, The Potato Eaters. I have seen this one in photos, but had no idea what a powerful painting it is. I cannot stop looking at it. Behind a divider is his Bedroom at Arles and the colors are so bright and unusual it is actually hard to look at. After seeing the original, you realize it has never been reproduced properly.

I walk around the other side of the divider and stop dead in my tracks. There it is, Crows Above a Cornfield, his final painting before he killed himself. The paint is so thick you can see every brushstroke on the canvas. It looks like a five year old made it while having a raging fit, but the emotion it conveys is of someone who has lived a thousand lifetimes. The crows and the bedroom, the sunflowers and the doctor, the gardens and the potato eaters, it all becomes overwhelming. I have to leave.

Chris finds me outside on a bench. I am trying to explain to him what happened in there. I think he understands. It feels like I have been given the ability to read books by just looking at them, and then am locked in a library overnight. Eventually you have to just close your eyes or you will go mad. It is all too much.

I have only seen a few Van Goghs up to this point, a few in D.C., some in Boston and a few scattered around during my travels. But, to have so many in one place at one time, it is too much for me to take in. I want to see as many of his works as I can before I die. This makes me feel that much closer to death.

The gift shop is huge and packed with wall to wall posters and postcards and calendars of his work. As we try to agree on something we can buy that won't get destroyed during the rest of the trip, Chris notices how ironic it is to hear all the cash registers continually ringing when you realize he never sold a painting during his lifetime. Did people just not understand what he was doing, which would make him a pioneer of his time, or is his lack of an easy life and struggle with impending madness part of what draws people to feel so passionate toward him? I think, for me, it is a little of both.

Walking the streets once again, we find ourselves in areas so full of people that it takes us a good half-an-hour to go a block. It is nothing but a sea of heads walking in every direction and breathing alcohol-laced breath on each other. We finally arrive at a less crowded courtyard and through an alleyway, we hear the sound of hundreds of people shouting. We follow the noise and find ourselves in the middle of a rally.

There are red and white flags being waved by the masses of people and matching banners hanging down the front of the buildings. On the balcony of the main building is a man with a microphone who is shouting something to the crowd, who in turn holler and wave and jump up and down. The ones on the rooftops of parked cars seem especially excited while the ones clinging to lampposts are doing there best not to fall.

The banners are red and the Dutch language, when shouted over a microphone, sounds a lot like German to those of us only schooled in English. I flash Chris a look of concern. Is this a neo-Nazi rally? Should I be scared? Should I even be here? The man next to us is wearing a suit and a dark pair of sunglasses. He holds his flag to the side and looks at me, a condescending smirk lounging across his face. He reminds me of what a KGB man should look like and I think I see a bulge in his jacket that somewhat resembles a gun with those bullets I am most likely allergic to.

We walk away from the mayhem and I find myself in front of a store window that is selling the same banners that the people are waving about.

73

The word AJAX is printed across the front. The name of their soccer team. This is a rally for the upcoming World Cup Tournament. They are not Nazis after all. Chris says he knew what it was all along. They are celebrating their team and have been for the last two days. As one can imagine, I feel like a complete idiot.

We go to the canal and watch the boats parade by. Many of them have dancing people on their rooftops wearing whatever costumes they could put together in their drunken stupor. We stop for a while on the side of the water and enjoy seeing if any of them will forget to duck when they float under the bridges. Across the canal is a crane with a bungee jumper hurtling toward his death, then he bounces, lives and the crowd erupts in cheers.

By afternoon, we are exhausted. Too many people, too much food and the ability to not find a chair to sit anywhere is getting annoying. We did find a good spot at one time and ordered our American Coca-Colas. They came with a lemon wedge inside and we thought this amusing. The lack of ice cubes I found less enjoyable. Sitting and drinking, we see a group of five men stop at the hedge next to our outside tables, put down there beers, take out their equipment and proceed to urinate on the hedges. I wonder if this is legal to do here. Chris says that it is legal to smoke pot, buy women and drink beer on the street, so why the hell not.

We decide to see a movie and head over to what we have deemed the Times Square of Amsterdam. It is full of large billboards and neon signs, advertising American and Japanese companies. There are two theatres to choose from, one has Schindler's List with an admission of Fl.20, and the other was playing Hot Shots Part Deux for a fee of Fl.2.50. If you had told me, I would be seeing Hot Shots while in Europe, I would have called you a liar.

It is fascinating that we can buy beer at the concession and excitedly take our glasses of brew and find seats. The movie is in English with Dutch subtitles. There is also subtitles in something that looks like Indonesian, though through the smoke of the moviegoers, it is really hard to tell what it is. Where America usually has sneak previews of coming attractions, this theatre plays commercials. They are the kind you would see on everyday television, but it is not just a few, they go on forever. I count around two hundred and fifteen before I give up. I am hoping they stop before my next birthday arrives.

To our joy, they play a short film of Mr. Bean. We are both big fans of Mr. Bean and this makes the whole thing worthwhile. The movie finally starts and we are amazed at all the different things that only the two of us find funny. There are some references that Europeans have not yet been exposed, like the Energizer Bunny, Bob Vila and The Clapper to name a few. While we laugh away at these, the rest of the audience sits in silence, smoking their cigarettes and drinking their beers.

The movie is wonderful and we are glad that at least the Dutch agree that overdubbing movies is a crime, instead using subtitles. Come to think of it, if life contained more subtitles, some people would be a lot easier to be around.

This is our last night in Amsterdam and I find that I am still intrigued with the Red-Light District. We decide to go back and window browse. First, I take my wallet back to the hostel. I do not really think I am the type to pay for any type of sexual favors, but my philosophy is, if you do not want to gamble, why walk into a casino with a pocket full of quarters?

The place is packed and we are laughing at the tour groups of geriatrics that have obviously signed up with some of Holland's more interesting tour companies. We watch transactions take place. We see people entering or leaving the little doors next to the windows. The windows themselves are provided with a curtain to pull over the front. One does not want to fornicate in front of vacationing grandmothers.

We find that the district is segregated in a way. The older women seem to be grouped together in one area and it seems that a lot of black women are congregated in another area. We wonder if this is by choice, on purpose or if it one of those things that just happens over time. After a couple of hours of walking, gawking, giggling and daydreaming, we decide to call it a night. When we get to the hostel, Chris says that he is going to say a prayer for all the lost souls. He then giggles himself to sleep.

Our bunks are in these huge dorms that must be holding at least sixty beds. They are bunk beds, so of course, Chris grabs the top one. There is a group of German guys sleeping next to us and in their leather jackets and spiked hair they look like they are coming back from a Billy Idol convention. I give Chris the alarm clock and ask him to wake me up in time for breakfast. I go to sleep with the sounds of at least ten people snoring. Normally this would give me the go ahead to make my nasal noise, but the Billy Idol's have intimidated me and I instead choose to sleep on my stomach, burrito style.

Chris forgets to wake me on time and I find myself having to scramble to get ready. This is no easy feat as I have to share six showers with sixty other guys, eight of which still look like Billy Idol. At breakfast, I meet a guy from Sweden who is thankful that he finally found a bed to sleep in. He says the first night he spent in a bar and the next two nights he slept in the lobby of a police station. I guess we did luck out after all. I eat my meal too fast and give myself the hiccups.

While looking around the hostel, I meet this guy Paul. He says he is from California, but has not been home for months. His parents are mad that he just took off like this, and except for their disappointment, he really has nothing else to go back to. He talked the hostel into letting him do odd jobs in exchange for a bed, and this arrangement has been working out nicely for a few weeks now. He has a return ticket to go back home, it leaves from Paris in three days. He does not have the money to make it to Paris and he would rather not go back home. We talk for a bit and I wish him luck. Something tells me he will still be here a month from now, and happy.

CHAPTER EIGHT

Bavaria
Coca-Cola, Sound of Music and Digestion

Past the makeshift camp of hippies and into the station, we catch the last train to Germany. The tulip fields of Holland are breathtaking. They look like someone has spread blankets of bright colors across the land. As we enter Germany, Chris is mesmerized with the scenery. We are rolling along the Rhine River and he is watching as the little towns pass below us, each with its own castle atop a hill. The country is amazingly lush and he says he only wants to be in a sports car right now, riding through the Rhine Valley, stopping to have lunch at a three-hundred-year-old inn and sampling the local wines. He is also thumbing through a comic book that he bought in Amsterdam. It is the Dutch version of X-Men, called De Xmannen.

I, on the other hand, am having a lousy train ride. The train is a little crowded and the only seat left in our compartment is facing backwards. I have tried to ride this way before and it always leads to my eventual bout with nausea. The conductor comes by, checks our tickets and then continues on. I get up, move into the next car, and find a forward facing seat. It is the smoking car, which also makes me ill, but in a much more tolerable way.

The conductor comes back through and starts checking tickets in the smoking car. When he asks for mine, I tell him that he already looked at it. In a loud voice, he says "Zeigen Sie mir ihre Fahrkarten!" I hand it to him. He notices he has already checked it and grunts in a way I can only assume is his way of admitting he is an idiot.

Half and hour later I am sitting with one of my feet up on the seat in front of me. I know this is not the way to treat other people's things, but I am tired and feel the need to elevate my leg for a while. The conductor comes by and yells at me for having my foot up. I make a show of wiping off the spot that I have apparently screwed up for future generations of train goers, but he still manages to glare at me on his way out of the car. Chris says part of the problem is that German is such a harsh language. He says they can say things like, isn't that cute or what a sweet puppy and it sounds like a death warrant. I am thinking it has to do with the fact that the conductor is an ass.

Not ten minutes later a woman asks me to please close my window. Okay, First, its hot in here, and two, it is my damn window! I slam it upward hoping she will feel the vibrations of my anger through the walls. Chris is amused at the fact that I am the one complaining right now.

Our train stops in Cologne for a second and we run out to look at the cathedral. It is very oddly built next to the train station, but impressive nonetheless. I am sure the church was here before the station was, but you would think those enjoying masses would rather not have the clanking of trains in the background. For some reason, I get excited to see a Burger King across the street and then a rude man bumps in to me without saying excuse me. I have decided I may not like Germany after all.

I make an effort to ignore the rest of Germany and borrow the Clive James book Chris bought earlier. I read the entire thing in less then three hours and this pisses him off to no end. He has had the book for over a week and he is barely on page eighty-five. He claims that I have inspired him to read and he finishes it before we reach our destination. His review of the book is that it was good, but he is not sure why it had to be told. My conclusion is much the same.

We arrive in Kempten late in the day and our host, Bart, is there to pick us up. Chris and Bart hit it off immediately. I can see the similarity in their personalities as we drive away from the train station. They both have that quiet, reserved thing going for them, but with a nice splattering of goofiness to boot. Bart and his family have been friends with Chris's family since the beginning of time. The kids spent summers together and each has pictures of the other decorating the walls of their houses.

They live in the cutest little town called Waltenhofen. It is in between two larger cities, but its isolation makes us feel like we are alone in the Bavarian countryside. As we turn off the main highway, I see a small village church and a field with cows. Could this be the Europe I have been searching for? Bart says that on a clear day, from their backyard, you can see the Alps.

We arrive at the house and his wife and daughter are here to greet us. I immediately take to his wife, Christa. Five minutes talking with her and I can tell she and I will have some great conversations in the coming days. She talks with a passion that intrigues me, though I think some of it is due to the fact that I have been conversing with Chris for the past half month. Not that he does not have passion, it is just, well, a little more subdued.

Tanja and Brian are their kids. They are twins, though the only way I can tell this is that Chris told me so. Brian is opinionated, funny and seems a lot like his mom. Tanja is more reserved and stubborn with a little bit of goofiness thrown in, like her dad. They are both athletic and attractive and would ensure the family did well should they enter a perfect-family contest.

We talk to the family for a bit, then Bart and Christa head off to bed. We stay up with Tanja, watch Beavis and Butthead on MTV Europe and eat white chocolate and Gummy Bears. Bob Vila and the Clapper haven't crossed the Atlantic, but Beavis and Butthead have? I think it all has to do with a good marketing team. Chris eventually drags himself to bed.

Tanja and I talk about MTV, movies and living in Bavaria. She knows a lot about America because they have visited there so often. I have no news to report to her since the last time she has visited. Life in Bavaria seems to be much like life anywhere else. They go to work, spend time with the family, watch television and try to figure out what to do with their free time.

Eventually we are yawning more than talking, so we say goodnight.

Our room is on the second floor and has one of those slanted roofs with a skylight built into it. The bed is actually two little beds pushed together to make one. We each have our own blanket and it seems enough like two beds to make Chris not bitch. I decide to lay down in my snoring position and apologize to Chris ahead of time, but he has already drifted off into a dream of Bavarian sheep, clean sheets and De Xmannen.

The next morning I wake up close to the crack of ten. Of course, Chris has already been up for hours and makes me look like a lazy bum. I find him downstairs and tell him I am hungry. He says he has left some bread and cheese for me on the kitchen counter.

Earlier that morning he had arrived in the kitchen to find Christa already up. He says that she asked him if he wanted her to get his breakfast or if he wanted to. He told her he would get it and then proceeded to wander around the kitchen, bumping into things. She made him sit down and she took care of it. He said he had a nice talk with her and he can see not only that her and Bart are complete opposites, but also, exactly what it is that attracts them to each other.

Christa comes in and asks what it is we like to eat. I start to name all the crap that composes my diet, Coke, pizza, taco bell, cheese, and the list goes on and on. Chris gives the more mundane answers that would make his mother proud to hear. Porridge, cereal, oat bran, vegetables, this coming from the guy that can put away Gummy Bears a pound at a time.

Then he makes the mistake of telling her that he really does not care what he eats. He says this is because the only reason he eats is for survival. The chewing and swallowing and waiting and digesting, he sees this all as a waste of time. Later he wonders if this was such a good thing to tell the person who will be cooking his future meals. I think my enthusiasm for food has more than made up for his indifference.

She heads off to the store and we decide to explore our Bavarian surroundings. The house is built next to a river, not near a river, next to a river. I could literally take a running jump off the porch and hit water. We decide to follow the river to see if we can get into trouble.

We find a small waterfall. It is small in the, not really big sort of way. However, if you were to try and boat off of it, I could guarantee that you would die or at least be hurt in a very bad way. We walk further and see a sign written in German that looks very menacing. I assume it is an early warning for the killer waterfall up ahead, but for all I know, it could be yelling at me to get my feet off the seat in front of me.

To our right is a field of yellow flowers. Chris decides that he wants to play Sound of Music. After making sure that I have camera at the ready, he runs into the field, arms out, spinning and hopping and twirling like an idiot. After this special moment has passed, we walk along the shore and I become excited when I find a big log. I heave it into the river with a strength that would make a Scotsman proud and then we proceed to bombard it with rocks. Chris says unless you are male, you probably would not understand the fun in this. Most likely, it just looks like we have a certain need to destroy things. I feel like I did when I was growing up in my small town. After a while, you learn to make your own entertainment, right Opey?

During dinner, I finally get to talk to Christa. She is magnificent. She reminds me of a quote by Charles Grodin, *"I am not much in to small talk."* She just gets down to it. We discuss religion in the family. I can see Chris is not really up to a deep theological discussion, but she gets me on a roll. She is saying that the parents should be in charge of religion until the kids are old enough to decide for themselves. This sounds logical to me, but of course, Bart, Chris and Tanja start to wail on about freedom to choose and cluttering the minds, etc. Brian jumps in and says that he agrees with us, and pretty soon, we have a very nice debate in the works. Oh, how I love a good debate.

After dinner, Bart retreats to the entranceway closet and returns bearing bottles of spirits. We each have a beer and it takes me a bit to get use to drinking it at room temperature. After we discuss more of life and its complexities, he opens a bottle of something blue that has a nice bit of crystallization happening on the inside. Christa jumps up to retrieve some small, silver glasses and he pours us each a shot. Chris says no thank you, but Christa insists this is the best thing to help with the process of digestion.

I have never had a problem with the process of digestion, but anything to assist my body in any of its functions I do with glee. I down this concoction in one swift movement and sit still as warmth in my belly slowly spreads throughout my body. Chris sees me drink and I know he feels the pressure of his peers. Christa tells him to go ahead and Bart tells her that if he does not want to he does not have to. I can tell this makes Chris feel like a wimp and he slams home the blue juice. If I was not already experiencing inner warmth, I know I would be at this moment, seeing Chris make a conscious effort to help with the process of his digestion.

CHAPTER NINE

Munich/Vienna
Apple Vendors, Kleptomania and Dictatorship

We wake up the next morning and pack our bags for Austria. Actually, we are stopping in Munich first, but saying that we are packing our bags for Munich does not sound as poetic for some reason. Either way, we are excited to be stuffing our packs with newly washed clothes. Knowing we will be wearing fresh items the next few days makes me whistle with glee.

I cannot say enough about European washers. The minute my underwear and socks come out of the washer they look whiter then they were when I bought them. We are thinking that we have somehow accidentally bleached the hell out of our clothes, but Christa explains to us that European washers fill themselves with water and then slowly become hot, extremely hot. It is kind of like making soup. Washing machines and the way toilets flush so forcefully are the two things I am most jealous of in this foreign land. Oh yeah, and also their sense of culture and history.

Our arms are sore from all the rock throwing yesterday, but since this is the most exercise we have had in a while, we only complain a little bit.

When we arrive for breakfast, there is a bottle of Coca-Cola on the table waiting for me. When she had asked us what we liked in the morning, she was serious. I was only telling her that I drank Coke for breakfast because I do, though I have been told its disgusting and unhealthy, I find it a crisp and refreshing way to start the day. So she went out and bought a crate of Coke. Now I feel guilty.

Don't get me wrong, I appreciate every last bubble of this sugary nectar. However, I can only imagine that buying a crate of imported American Coke, in Bavaria, probably cuts into the amount of heat they will be able to afford for the family next winter. She assures me it's fine and proceeds to pour. Coke in the morning is heaven in a glass to me, and if I can only explain to her that it needs to be chilled first, all will be well.

She drives us to the train station with the notion that we are late. I can only think that is the notion she has, or else, the brakes have given out and she is not telling us. We zoom through the countryside, pass other cars and I think we even cut off a train at one point. I feel safe smashed between the two backpacks in the back seat, but my head is exposed, and I am sure it is at least the third or fourth most vulnerable place on my body. We screech to a halt and I find that I have been doing a death-grip on the backpacks. I shall, next time she drives us to the station, nap during the trip.

We get a *be careful* speech that would make our mothers proud. We are left to begin another ride with Germany's finest. Brian told us last night that the train people are mean to everybody, so this makes me feel a little bit better. Of course, if this is proven to me by seeing Chris get a dose of the Germanic scolding, then I may be able to put it all behind me once and for all. I still think it has something to do with my long hair or the fact that I am wearing shorts. Prejudice knows no boundaries.

We arrive in Munich and wander the streets, trying to find a subway entrance. It has just finished raining and the city has that smell cities get, when everything becomes a little wetter but no cleaner. Wet dogs are a good example. We finally find the subway and get off where the hostel is supposed to be. We are at an entrance to a zoo, and though this makes us happy, it brings us no closer to a bed. Due to a lack of signs, the hostel remains hidden from us.

We wander up and down the street it is supposed to be on and I eventually break down and ask a man selling fruit if he knows where we need to go. He first points to the zoo and then offers to sell me an apple. Despite his helpfulness, I do not feel like I have gotten any closer to an answer. Finally, Chris says he thinks he has figured it out and we wander up a side road, sniffing the wet-dog air, wondering how we are going to know when we are lost.

Around a bend and through some low-hanging branches we see the hostel. It is an impressive structure from the outside and the inside looks like a purposeful mix of a YMCA and a Mormon temple. There is actually a large sculpture in the middle of the lobby and huge staircases that lead up to, what I can only imagine, are the honeymoon suites of the hostel world.

We book two beds, but find out that even though the beds are only twenty-six and a half Deutsche Marks, the deposit is twenty Deutsche Marks. They do not accept travelers checks and they do not accept credit cards. I assume that they do not like losing the interest one pays when these items are cashed at a bank. Personally, I do not like losing the interest either. Chris makes a very profound observation. He says that these youth hostels do not make things as easy as they think they do.

We go back to town to find a bank. On the way out, Chris notices that the zoo is suppose to have penguins. We are not planning to go to the zoo, but this bit of information seems to cheer him up a bit. I need to store this in the back of my head for later. If I ever need to apologize for something, I can just go out and buy Chris a little penguin thing, or at least make cute penguin noises until he forgives me.

The bank screws us on the interest and we return to the hostel. The fruit man tries to wave me down but I ignore him as best I can. Our rooms are on the fourth floor. We go up in an elevator and I realize this is the first one I have been in since our trip began. I do not think this is a commentary on European conveniences. I just think we have been visiting places that are vertically lacking. Our room has four beds in it and we are anticipating what our roommates will be like.

I feel like I am in a football locker room. The walls and furniture are blue and orange and give it a *Go Team* atmosphere. Everything is very clean and very neat and even the bathroom being at the end of the hall does not seem like an inconvenience. No one else arrives and we assume the room is ours alone. We wake up to find no one in the other two beds, but one of them has a towel draped over it. I can only assume we have slept with ghosts who like to shower.

We skip breakfast and head into Munich. Our first stop is the Museum of Science and Industry. This place is enormous and we are too excited that they have allowed us in. Each floor is divided into sections, all celebrating the inventions of cars, boats, rockets, airplanes and everything else that was thought up at one time or another.

The whole place is a hands-on museum, with buttons to push, wheels to turn and handles to crank. Chris is most excited to see the planes and jets that are scattered throughout. I am more than happy to play with the glowing balls that make my hair stand up.

We learn how tunnels are dug, bridges are built and how a dam is constructed. I get to play on a contraption that weighs different parts of my body and my head is somewhere between five and eight pounds, thought I think my neck may have been helping more than it will admit, or my head is somewhat lighter than the average head, which is a little scary when you think about it. I jot this information in my journal in case it should come up later. You never know. Chris has also learned quite a bit. He now knows how the footings for bridges are placed. We spend the entire day in here and even manage to sneak up to the roof at one point and have a nice, birds-eye view of the city.

Eventually the museum closes and they kick us out. The thought of hiding and being locked in here is tempting, but we figure they probably let dogs loose at night, and what fun would that be.

Outside is a man making Crepes. He is cleaning up to go home, but the look of hunger on our faces must get to him, because he agrees to make us some. They are a concoction of tomato sauce, ham and cheese. These are the best things I have ever eaten. *Ever!* (You see, this is what happens when you skip breakfast).

We decide the next best thing to do is go to a beer-garden, or Biergarten, as the locals call it. Unfortunately, it starts to rain again and we decide that it is no longer beer drinking weather, at least not outside in some garden anyway. We make our way back to the subway, taking turns trying to remember the words to the songs in When Harry Met Sally.

Near the subway, there is a giant sculpture of two cows, or maybe they are oxen, standing near a waterfall. I cannot figure out if it is a tribute to livestock, farmers or just something they thought would look nice near a waterfall. Either way, Chris has decided that he wants a picture with them and clamors atop one of the beasts. He is very high up and very visible in his green and yellow jacket, waving at me to take his picture. Afraid that we will have to apologize to a police officer for this behavior, I hurriedly take his picture and yell at him to get down. One more cool picture for Chris, Damn!

We walk some more, crossing over the river that divides the city. On the bridge, there is an awesome view of the capital building that is reminiscent of what one would see in D.C. The riverbanks are overflowing with green trees. The water is reflecting the gray sky above and the rain has stopped long enough for me to be able to capture this moment on film. We decide that the Crepes did not do their jobs and end up in a McDonalds. This is the first time we discover they serve beer in McDonalds.

We are off to Vienna tomorrow. The check out time is nine in the morning, which sounds early after being able to sleep in at the Termonds. I wake up with enough time to eat breakfast. Our routine is that I shower first and then head to breakfast, Chris likes to head for breakfast and then cleanse himself. I have to have my shower first, otherwise I am too nervous that time will run out. Not being able to bathe, to me, is the type of tragedy I do not like to even think about. Chris likes to make sure he has his morning meal before the day begins. I guess this shows exactly where our priorities lie.

The breakfast is amazing. I am in a cafeteria with hundreds of other backpackers. There is a line for trays and the food is spread out like a buffet. They have cereals, eggs benedict, porridge and fruit. They even have a woman who is passing out small cartons of milk and juice. It feels weird to sit with a table full of people I do not know, but after we exchange pleasantries, it is apparent that most of them have not eaten this well in a while. We dig in with smiles on our faces. After everyone has started eating, a nice woman walks around with a bucket full of oranges. I tell her no thank you, but she insists I take one, for later in the day. The coffee is weak, but four cups of it later, I feel like I can face my day.

Due to a lack of speed on my roommate's part, we miss the first train to

Vienna and have to hang out for an extra half an hour. I inform him that he has started the day on my shit list. I soon forgive him though as our train turns out to be very clean and very empty. We ride through an amazing green landscape, the overcast skies making it even more picturesque. The conductor is a very nice man. He stamps our passports and then tells us thank you. This train ride has undone all the evils of earlier German train rides. Of course, there is a slight possibility this is a loaner train from Sweden and the Germans just forgot to tell them how to blend in.

Chris has decided that his wisdom teeth are coming out. He says the right side of his mouth is really hurting, especially when he bites into hard bread crust. He also thinks he is developing a sore throat, which he attributes to either sleeping with his mouth open or drinking coke instead of water for days on end. He adds to this the fact that he burnt his tongue this morning. He drank some tea that was scalding hot, but instead of spitting it out in front of a cafeteria full of people, he forced it down his throat. Thinking it over, he has also decided that the left side of his mouth hurts. Perhaps, he says, something has ruptured.

Normally this type of complaining drives me nuts, only because I am the one that likes to do it. He is making me laugh though. There is an air of creativity about it and he seems to be enjoying the fact that he is pushing on despite these near-debilitating afflictions. I rally to his side and he makes it apparent he can go on, the poor dear.

Vienna is exactly the way you see it in postcards. Well, not exactly. It is not contained within a 3x5 square piece of paper with scribbles of gibberish on the backside, but you get my drift.

The hostel here is reasonable and we have a very nice room with two guys from Canada. They are not traveling together but seem to be on friendly terms with each other. It is nice to share a room with others who speak English as a first and only language. I think Chris likes it because he can make conversation and find out interesting places to go. I like it because in order for them to say anything impolite about things like my snoring or the way that I part my hair, they will have to do it in whispers.

One of the Canadians, Jeff, is spending all of his time going to Vienna's ballets, operas and symphonies. He has a million brochures of upcoming events that he offers us to look through. The other guy, Lars, is in the middle of a trip through Eastern Europe and is on his way out tomorrow morning.

After surviving on train food most of the day we ask them if they have any suggestions where to go eat. I am hoping they will not inform us that there is a McDonalds just down the street. Of course, if they did, I would probably just walk over there like a zombie and order whatever meal looks like it will add to my girth the quickest. They give us directions to a place called Der Tunnel, actually it is just called Tunnel, but I call it Der Tunnel because that sounds more exotic to my ears.

It is a cute little restaurant, with pub style tables. The only light provided is from the slowly sinking sun. The waitress is nice enough and actually brings us water with a couple of ice cubes floating on top. I assume that she can either tell we are Americans or they are trying to slowly defrost their freezer out back.

It is still around brunch time, but Chris orders Meat Spaghetti and a beer. I have Pasta Carbinara, which is covered with a cream sauce and makes my taste buds stand up and cheer. I down a Cappuccino with my meal and realize this is the first real coffee I have had in days. My insides give me a few knocks of approval.

After our meal, we wander around the city for a while. Chris thinks, for a big city, it is remarkably friendly. I think the language is too close to stern-German for them to be able to withhold being rude to me for much longer. Perhaps it is a race thing. No one has been able to figure out what I am. The guesses have ranged from Italian to Eskimo to Spanish, French to Italian to Native American. I like to think of myself as a representative of the world, which probably makes me prime pickings for other world beings looking for earth samples. Egads!

We walk around for a while, and to my surprise, Chris gets lost. I would say we get lost, but I was lost five minutes after we left the restaurant. He pulls out the map and sets us straight. Now we are back to an organized and respectable stroll. I soon forget which way is north and am confused as to why all the streets are going in circles. A familiar, happy glow spreads over me as I realize I am lost again.

We stop at a post office, and even though the rates are still high enough to make Chris angry, we exchange some money. For the most part, I am just glad to be able to exchange my money for theirs. I figure that if they wanted to, they could make us bring gifts of livestock and wheat, in order to have some of their money. Anything that saves me from having to steal from outlying farms is a good deal to me. I usually wait until afterwards to find out how much they ripped me off and then complain that we should have looked a little harder for a better deal.

Chris, on the other hand, has brought with him this cute little calculator that can actually figure out the exchange rates of most countries. A little part of each day is spent watching him look at the exchange rate posted in a bank, punch his little keyboard furiously and then say an explanative. I still have not figured out why they screw me so much just to trade money. I suppose it is because they know I have no choice, and when I am left with no choices, I will most likely give in to anything. But do not spread that around.

As we enter St. Stephen's Cathedral, a guy at the door tells us that we are not allowed to come in here with shorts on or exposed shoulders. I glance at our pant-covered legs and Chris takes a peek at our shirt-covered shoulders. I can only assume this guy did something stupid, went to confession and his absolution requires him to annoy me.

The church has no lights and the only way to make our way around is by the light streaming through the stain-glass windows. There is a ton of stain-glass windows, which I assume is the whole point of this absence of electricity. Instead of the cheesy tourist shop we have gotten used to seeing in the back of churches, there is a shelf of postcards with a box to drop money in. Could this be the honor system? That seems so inappropriate in this day and age. I can only assume that somewhere behind a stone cherub, there is an infrared camera with recording capabilities, aimed at these tempting goods.

We go take a look at Hofburg Palace, the Church of St. Charles and then on to Stadtpark. Here, Chris decides to indulge in his first Bratwurst, ever. He likes it, but thinks that maybe the hot mustard is too much. I decide to not indulge in a large sausage at this time. I am watching my figure. Trying to stay lean and trim. I find some nice looking fountains and sit down to sketch them. I have somehow lost my ability to draw anything that does not look like I am suddenly suffering from an extremely bad case of hand arthritis. I eventually give up.

Across from Karlspark, Vienna's largest square, is the Künstlerhaus. Chris assumes this translates to art house, but I can only shrug and tell him he is probably right. To be honest, Chris has told me the name of everywhere we have been today. For all I know, the churches we have visited could all be named Danforth. He likes to carry the European travel books that tell him the facts about this and that and what to see in each city. I tried this in the beginning, but when I find they are telling me things like how tall the windows are and what the caretaker had for breakfast, I start thinking I am getting just a bit too much information.

I will admit though, if I did not have Chris and his common sense approach to traveling, I would probably still be trying to figure out which subway line to take to get out of London. Of course, I do not tell him this. Instead I act like I am a free spirit, letting the wind take me where it does, and let him have the pleasure of pointing out that this door was made from a three-thousand year old boat and that bell tower was the setting for many Eighteenth-century, pastoral debaucheries. He wants to be a teacher someday, and I am considering myself a student of the world, and with this load of bullshit in my head, we continue on our way.

Within the Künstlerhaus is a show called Art and Dictatorship. It is a collection of drawings, paintings, posters and architecture that have to do with dictators throughout Europe's history. Seeing the banner out front, with a picture of Lenin standing strong and proud, it seems this is less a show of historical items and more a celebration of the role of Dictators.

Maybe I would be more receptive to it if they called it The Dictator and the Bad Stuff They Did, or The Dictator, Rulers That Oftentimes Did Not Need the 'tator' at the End of Their Titles. It could also be the fact that they have a statue at the foot of the entrance that is most becoming. It is a dictator, standing proudly in his ornate robe. Beneath him is a naked, bald man, holding on to its folds, trying to pull himself up. Nice image.

Chris is excited to go in. To him this is an important part of history. I tell him I refuse to spend my money to support something like dictatorship. I know the money is not going to any sort of dictator college scholarship fund, but to me this is as bad as going to an art instillation about Nazism. I do not see the problem of showing what happened to their victims, mainly to ensure it will never happen again, but to profit off of the unrealized dreams of madmen, this bugs me too much.

After a while I talk myself into a whirl of confusion, the noise I am making is just noise. None of it makes any sense to me anymore, but I decide to stand by my convictions. I will stay outside and draw the statue across the street and the church down the road. Sometimes I wonder if I am being too opinionated about things.

Before he heads in I decide that maybe I have gone overboard on this thing, but it looks like Chris is more than happy to go in without me. In fact, he seems very happy to be going in without me. I wonder if he has reached the point of being tired of me yet. I have to admit, he has gotten on my nerves every now and then, but I still think we are doing pretty good for two people that are spending more time together than Siamese cellmates.

He says he thinks we are getting to the point where we like the cities better than we like each other. That seems like not such a bad thing, unless of course, we should stumble upon an amazingly attractive city with nice attributes and one of us is unlucky enough to find the other has eloped.

After Chris is done with the dictators, we head over to the Opera House. He does not talk much about the museum, but mentions that it was very well done and he wishes they had put a gift shop at the end. I cannot think of what they would sell at such a gift shop, except for some key chains that say Oppress Others, and possibly a book or two entitled Dictating For Dummies.

The Opera House has the last tour of the day gathering near the door, and we decide to join them. Waiting to go on our tour is a gang of overly-caffeinated teenagers. We are both magically transported back to the night train from Edinburgh to London. We decide we do not need to see the Opera House after all.

I was never that irritating in my youth. They should have given awards in grade school for not being an idiot instead of perfect attendance. I think it would be better to not show up all the time and be a nice person, rather than have perfect attendance and then bug everyone that is there with you. As you can tell I am a little upset that we let obnoxious, underage hyenas ruin a chance to see the Opera House, but the knowledge that they will some day get older, have to pay rent and work boring jobs makes me feel a little bit better.

The sky is a nice overcast and we wander some more. There are a lot of horse-drawn carriages here and they seem mainly to be catering to the tourist trade. I almost want to get on one, but it seems to lose that special Dr. Zhivago-ness when I picture myself sitting next to Chris in the soft light of dusk. Not that Chris is a bad catch. I would just prefer to tour a major European city, on the back of a carriage, with someone that fits into the category of not being a man.

Chris has noticed that there is a lot less traffic here than anywhere we have been. This makes him happy knowing that he does not have to be dodging cars every time he crosses a street. I wonder if the inordinate amount of horse droppings on the road has been a factor in any of this.

We decide we are hungry again. For someone not interested in food, I notice Chris gets hungry often. Of course, I am no one to talk. Eating a hearty meal can, in itself, give me an appetite. We head back to Der Tunnel. We love the food, the prices are good and this is the best way to ensure we will not be putting any more of old man McDonald's kids through college.

Chris has a Pizza Margharita Klein, which is cheese pizza for one. I have a Pasta Bologna and a Kaartoast. I expect something called a Kaartoast to be a five-foot long loaf of bread, sliced down the middle and toasted with cheese, garlic and oregano in the center. What it turns out to be is a cheese sandwich. I am slightly disappointed until I learn that my pasta will not actually be having little bits of Bologna in it, and then I am okay again. I decide I want a trinket from this place and Chris suggests perhaps a sugar packet or a napkin, but I have already focused on the item I want to take home. It is the ashtray on our table.

The ashtray is made of glass and has the names of different Austrian beers labeled on it. Chris points out that I cannot just take an ashtray, but I inform him that the acquirement of said ashtray will be as much fun as the having. I open my little backpack on the floor and put it on the side of the table. When our waitress is out of sight, one swoop sends the ashtray flying into my bag. Chris says we are going to get caught and thrown in jail for this type of behavior. After a couple of minutes, I decide he is probably right, but am not able to find an opportunity to place it back on the table. I am forced to keep this object that will one day be an item of Austrian history. I wish I had checked to see if there were any ashes in it.

Our discussion turns toward what we think of Europe so far. I explain to

Chris that I am a little disappointed that it has not lived up to what I was expecting to find. He is curious, so I explain. To me, Europe is supposed to be walking through beautiful countryside, working for our daily meals and sleeping in whatever barn or haystack the people will provide for us. In short, I wanted to have an Of Mice and Men journey, but without the problems or the poverty. I pictured horse-drawn carriages, men on stilts lighting street lamps, pubs that serve drinks in wooden steins and women that wear dresses that make their bosoms look like they are being introduced to me.

Of course, Chris tells me I am an idiot and about a hundreds years too late. He points out that I would probably get pissed after one day having to work for my food and that I already bitch enough when I have to sleep in a bed that could use a newer mattress. A horse-drawn carriage is not entirely impossible to find and he is sure the women of Amsterdam's Red-Light District would have been glad to introduce their bosoms to me. As far as the rest of it is concerned, I am pretty much screwed.

Chris tells me that he thinks this form of travel is fine, but he admits he would rather do it as a vacation. His definition of a vacation is the ability to fly into the city you want to stay, get a nice hotel, go on tours and mainly just sit around and send postcards. He is tired of carrying everything on his back and sleeping in a room with people that he would not even look at photographs of.

In a way, I can understand where he is coming from, but in another way I am hoping this is only his tiredness talking. I would hate to think this experience is the last of its kind for him. Mainly because I know he will think back on these days with fondness and partially because I need to ensure I will have someone stupid enough to do this with me again in the future.

On our way back to the hostel, we pass by a little ice cream shop. They have freezers full of those ice cream drumsticks and we decide that life cannot go on before we have one of those. The woman running the shop is very excited to see us and says only one word the entire time, Wunderbar! Everything is Wonderful! We would like some ice cream. Wunderbar! Here is the money. Wunderbar! Have a good night. Wunderbar! Chris is excited because I am the only person he has heard say that up until this time. I am happy because I know he thought I was making the word up until now. I love it when I am accused of dishonesty and then I am vindicated, it just feels Wunderbar!

Chris says there is a concert tonight that we should think about going to. We get back to the hostel and decide to kick back for a little while. I fool myself into thinking I am going to write beautiful prose in my journal, describing the land and its people. Instead, my body decides it wants me to fall asleep to see how much I can drool in an hour's time.

Chris wakes me up to go to the festival. I am not use to taking naps and hate the groggy feeling I get afterwards. I think I make threats on his life if this thing is not worth my having to stop slobbering uncontrollably. I am pretty sure he brushes my threats aside, like he does most other things I say to him.

Chris says this festival is called the Wiener Festwochen. Of course, I think this means the Festival of the Weenies, until I remember that Wiener is the same word as Vienna. The main stage is in front of the Capital Building. The building shines a fantastic white from the lights that hit it from every angle. The seats on the side and the back are filling rapidly, but we notice the ground in front of the stage still looks rather empty.

We find ourselves just feet in front of the stage. The area behind us slowly fills in and soon an air of excitement takes over the crowd. A man comes out and says some words that I am sure everyone else understands as they laugh, cheer or holler in unison. After he leaves, the orchestra plays a couple of songs for us.

A bit later, a group of men and women come out and perform a musical. It is in German, making it seem both serious and scary to me, but the crowd seems to approve so I do not feel the need to run. After they finish there is a long pause as they let the excitement of the crowd grow. When the buzz is deafening, a man comes out and introduces the two people that will be performing tonight's opera. The woman's he introduces as Agnes, to which the crowd goes wild and Chris and I feel stupid for not knowing who she is. Then they introduce her partner, and he has a very familiar sounding name, something like Placido Domingo.

The place erupts and my eyes and mouth are about the same size in circumference. I turn to Chris and exclaim what an amazing surprise this is.

He tells me that Placido was listed on tonight's program. He says that he told me this, but I do not remember and rejoice in the surprises my lack of knowledge has brought to my day. Placido and Agnes are magnificent as they sing three songs each. Chris says that at one point, when Placido was at a crescendo, the wind picked up and blew his coat tails behind him. He said it could not have been more perfect if it had been staged for a movie.

I did not notice this because I was too busy watching the guy in front of us. He is only five feet tall and looks to be pushing his late eighties, but fought his way to the foot of the stage. He dances to every tune, knows the words to every song and generally just sways his smiling, hairless head from side to side. I do not think I have seen anyone have more fun anywhere. After Placido belts out his last tune, an important city official present he and Agnes with some type of award and then a troop of ballet dancers take over the stage. After they twirl, leap and pirouette, the Blue Danube Waltz is performed and this signals the end of the festivities.

We mingle with the crowd for a while and then Chris remembers he is hungry. We search for a place to get an apple strudel, but this is not a strudel crowd, so we have no luck. Instead, we get two very large beers and a thing called a lango, which looks like a giant elephant ear and tastes like fry bread with a lot of brown sugar on it.

This night we sleep well. The songs of Placido are still twirling around our heads and the giant, sugary elephant ears lay contently in our stomachs. Vienna turns out to be better than I expected and all that Chris has hoped. Tomorrow we head into the Czech Republic, and Prague, the place I have wanted to see more than any other.

CHAPTER TEN
Prague

Kafka's Grave, Bob Marley and Little Bird

We are on the overnight train to Prague. We did not book a bed car, mainly due to the fact that neither of our fathers is the CEO of any major corporations, thus our funds limit us to riding coach. We are in a regular coach car that is made to seat six people. Luckily, instead of having a room full of people staring at each other's heads, it is just the two of us. We take this opportunity to spread out. It is an interesting ride as the lights never go off, the train is loud and the ticket guys bug us every time we stop at another depot. Other than that, we are just tired and uncomfortable.

The night becomes more so, and we eventually lay across the seats that God has seen fit to provide us, but the conductor comes by and yells at us to sit up. Being resourceful youths, we figure out that by putting our legs straight out onto the seat in front of us, it feels enough like a bed (minus the butt support) to put us to sleep.

We are semi-happily nodding off to the vibrations of the train rolling beneath us when the conductor comes in again and tells us that we have to sit up correctly. He says we did not pay for a sleeper car so we do not lie down like we have one. Apparently, we have to suffer for the fact that his wife is withholding sex from him. I knew Austrians were too much like Germans for them to be kind to me for long.

Earlier in the day, Chris mentioned that the Eurail pass did not seem to actually cover our ride to the Czech Republic. He said maybe it would be okay, since the only way to get from Austria to Berlin would be to go through this region, so we would have to go this way regardless. Our rail map doesn't actually say that it does not cover the Czech Republic, it just shows the rail line in red up to the border, then when it hits this region it turns gray, and then when it leaves this region it turns red again. If we ignore the legend on the left side of the map, this could be a printing mistake for all we know.

I suggest to him that we are on an overnight train, meaning the train workers will most likely be sleeping or in the bar car drinking the vodka. Also, if they really had a problem with it, they would stop the train before allowing us to so easily enter such a forbidden region. The train does stop at one point, in a small town that is below the Czech border, but it looks like a normal stop and no one announces we have to disembark. Of course, even if they had made such an announcement, I would have stayed put. Heaven knows the last thing I need is to be wandering small border towns in the middle of the night.

We eventually decide to take the wrath of the conductor and lay our weary heads upon our seats. Being on a train at night makes it possible to do only two things, sleep or solve murders. It appears we are doing fine as the conductor passes by the door several times without looking in on us. Perhaps he thinks we have disembarked or perhaps he has decided to leave us alone. Maybe his wife is ovulating and told him to hurry home.

It is four in the morning when the door to our compartment opens and two men enter. Neither of them is Austrian. These men have on dark, blue uniforms and appear to be Czech.

We immediately sit up to show that we are not, in fact, using the seats as beds. Neither of them seems concerned with this. The younger of the two asks to see our passports and the older one plays the part of the tough, quiet friend.

We give him our passports and our Eurail passes. After looking them over for a bit, he confers with the older man for a while. The older man's voice has a menacing sound to it. I cannot help but think the worst. The younger one bends to me and shows me the map of the region. He traces the rail line and points out the obvious. The red line turns gray. I try to look confused and then surprised, but I do not know if he was able to appreciate my performance in this light.

Chris is looking at me and his eyes are either saying *oh shit* or *your fault*. It is not exactly my fault, but even if it is, what is the worst they could do to us anyway? The older guy leaves the compartment for a minute and the younger guy tells us it will be just a minute. He does not hand our passports or rail passes back to us and I wonder if this is because they need something to identify the bodies with later.

After a few minutes, a third man is brought in. He looks nice and speaks remarkable English. He tells us that our tickets are not valid to enter the Czech Republic and we will have to purchase tickets to continue on this train. We are relieved that the remedy is this non-violent, but concerned at what a train ticket will cost us. We have been calculating the trips we have taken, and have realized that without this Eurail pass, we would have had to stay put in Den Haag for a month. Tickets from point to point are quite expensive in Europe, even if the cities are only a thumbnail apart on the map.

He figures out what we owe and writes down the amount. Chris takes out his calculator and does the math. They are asking the exurbanite amount of seven dollars apiece. It turns out this third guy is an exchanger of money and he gives us Czech Krones for our Austrian Shillings. We remember what my friend Nicole had told us about the Czech Republic. Apparently, since the fall of communism, the Czech economy has been doing crazy things. She was in Prague not a month ago and remembered drinking thirty-cent pints of beer and staying at hotels for under ten dollars a night. To them, seven dollars was a lot of money, to us, it was seven dollars. We thank them for not killing us, take back our essentials and lay down on our makeshift beds. Tomorrow we wake up in Prague, city of a hundred spires.

We arrive into town during the early morning hours. The platform is full of people who are waiting for the train and there is one man in particular that is apparently waiting for us. He is wearing a periwinkle shirt, blue jeans and a thick pair of glasses. He is a step or two ahead of us, talking to us in German. Chris thinks we look German because he is no longer wearing his white look-at-me-I-am-American sneakers. I am thinking it is because I look grumpy, in a, someone is putting there feet up on a train seat, kind of way.

Either our confused looks or lack of response make the man realize we are not German. He immediately switches to broken English. The man with the broken English tells us that he has an apartment if we want to rent it from him. He says he can take us to it and if we do not like it, we do not have to stay. Chris and I slow down to hold a quick conference. We both hate hostels at this point and having an apartment in Amsterdam had been very enjoyable. Chris says he feels uncomfortable about this but I counter with the fact that we can easily beat this man up if we have to.

We tell him we will take a look at it and he happily leads us to the subway. He pays for our subway tickets, which I think is weird, but then remember that he is trying to make a sale. On the subway, he sits next to me, leaning in to tell me his facts. His name is Lubos something, and though I could never pronounce his last name, he says it means little bird in Czech. To emphasize this he makes a little bird hand gesture.

He seems really nice and I am not at all nervous about going with him, but what does bother me is his breath is noxious as hell. It smells like a goat died underneath his tongue. I am trying to lean away from him and praying that our stop comes soon. We finally stop at the other side of town. Where we exit has a Czech name, two words starting with P. That is all that stays with me and will have to be enough to get me home should we become separated.

We follow him to an apartment building and I so happily lug my backpack up four flights of stairs. The building does not have an elevator, but what it lacks in convenience, it more than makes up for in peeling paint. At this point, it hits me that this would be the perfect set up for bad guys. First you lead the foreigners to an empty apartment and have three big goons waiting to beat us up and steal our stuff. Of course, I think of this after I have made it to the top of the third floor and am willing to risk bodily injury rather than go back down.

The apartment is a handsome little number. It is a studio, consisting of one big bed, a kitchenette and a chair. There is a bathroom to one side and a balcony on the other. No one is in here to beat me up and this gives it a nice ambiance. He says that it is his apartment and he rents it out to make extra money. He will be staying at a friend's house.

His asking price is a little more than the hostel, but we would get our own bathroom, so we decide to stay. We pay him for one night and he says that if we want to stay longer, to leave the money in a kitchen drawer that he will check every day. If he does not find any money, he will assume that we no longer want to stay. He hands us the keys and bids us farewell.

Chris is amused that we have our own bathroom. He is surprised because he saw this film once, in grade school, about people in Russia living in one room of an apartment building full of hundreds of families. The one bathroom was in the basement, for all to use. He knows it was about Russia and he knows it was during the Cold War, but there is some kind of point he is trying to make and I am unable to tell what the hell it is.

We do notice that there is a lack of toilet paper to use, but as luck would have it, I have my traveler's emergency toilet paper for just such an occasion. No one can say that I do not take things seriously. Chris is thinking that maybe he should write an essay about our toilet paper adventures, calling it Toilet Paper and the Grand Cities of Europe.

We change clothes, lock our bags to the bedpost and head out into the world of the Czech. Lubos (little bird) has told us that our subway tickets are good for one hour, so we assume we can at least get downtown before they expire. As we waltz down the stairway to catch our train, a man in a purple sweatshirt says something to me in Czech. I am assuming he is trying to borrow some money or wants to sell me a can opener, so I say no thanks and continue on down. Chris stops for him because he can tell the man is serious about something. I head back up and he asks to see our subway tickets. After looking them over, he then asks to see our passports and we hand them to him like a couple of idiots. He walks to the entrance of the subway and we follow. He tells us read the signs.

To our amazement, they are written in English. We have not seen English since London, so assuming we won't ever again, we do not bother to even look at signs unless they seem to be warning us about killer waterfalls. The signs tell us that our subway tickets are good for one hour, but only in the subway. If you leave for any reason, they become invalid. Lubos (little bird) forgot to mention this part.

I tell the man we are sorry, thinking that it is not only obvious that we did this on accident, but that we are foreigners and therefore slightly stupid. What is his reply to this? He says, "Sorry does not do no good, you are going to have to pay."

Sorry does not do no good? What the hell is that? Then the jerk makes us pay a fine for breaking his idiotic, bullshit rules. We do not really feel like we have a choice, as this purple-shirt monkey is holding our passports. We have to keep from smiling as he hits us with a fine amount of seven dollars and ten cents.

There must be something about breaking the law here, in relation to seven dollars. Though subway tickets are only twenty-four cents, the seven dollars still seems like a small amount to part with. We give this chimp cash, which he puts into his pocket and then hands back our passports. He tries to give us one of those hard looks that say now don't let me catch you doing this again, but all that his beady, little eyes convey to us is that he has never really come to grips with the fact that he's a small man, in both stature and content.

On our way down the stairs, Chris is cursing under his breath. He says that when that jerk asked for our passports, we should have kicked him in the shins, pushed him down the steps and left the country. I bet you anything that the money we paid him is going toward a hooker or a gambling debt or whatever else this guy does on his days off.

We get on the train and Chris finds he is fascinated with the Prague subways. He likes that each station is announced loud enough for us to hear, even if we cannot tell what the hell they are saying. He says it is the thought that counts. He also likes the fact that the drivers are maniacs. They go from being perfectly still to driving a hundred and fifty two miles an hour in a matter of three or four seconds. We found the most fun is to be had while staring out the door at the front of the car. Watching the other cars twist and turn ahead of ours makes for an amusing ride.

For me, Prague officially wins as the coolest city in the world. It is full of canals, bridges, castles and cobblestones. It is exactly the Europe I was dreaming of. The city is amazing to look at from a distance, with all the steeples and spires jutting into the sky. When you are in it, it transports you back at least a century or two. We check out a few places that we need to hit while here, mainly the post office and a bank.

We walk to the river and look over the side. There is a huge, concrete embankment on our side, at least sixty feet wide and we notice some tables and chairs underneath the bridge. A long staircase takes us to the bottom, and to a café, that serves beer out of one window and coffee out of another. We order beer from a lady that services both windows and then go sit at a table. Not ten seconds later the same lady stomps up to our table. She folds her arms and says, "No beer, go!"

I notice that the tables are divided into two sections, those in front of the coffee window and those in front of the beer window. The beer window seating is all filled up, and despite the fact that the coffee window seating is empty and a mere six inches away, these are apparently not suited for our alcoholic ways. I point out to her that there are no seats in the beer section, but she does not want to have any discussions about it.

Milling around like idiots we finally give up on the fact that we are going to find a seat in the beer section. We walk to the edge of the river and sit with our legs dangling over. Luckily, she lets us sit here and finish our beers. This is probably because she has such a kind heart.

On our way back to the apartment, we are stopped by yet another man, who asks to see our subway tickets. This time we know the scoop and he looks disappointed that he cannot humiliate us. He then spots two other people with backpacks and immediately yells at them to show their tickets. These jerks are only stopping tourists. How nice is that? Then, when he is not able to steal their money, he turns around and shrugs to another man across the terminal. We turn to see to whom he is shrugging, and lo' and behold, it is our little friend from earlier today. Chris says he hopes these guys were beaten as children.

The next morning we are up at an hour normally set-aside for paper-delivery boys. We wander into town and look at everything in the daylight. The city itself is almost beyond words. The main strip, Wenceslas Square,

I remember seeing in documentaries. It was when thousands of people were gathering around the statue of St. Wenceslas, during the Velvet Revolution of 1989. We find a café for breakfast and order Crepes. Chris gets the one that has fruit in the middle and mine has scrambled eggs.

The train tickets, the beer seating and the subway guy are the three things that have introduced us to Prague. Luckily, the surroundings make up for the people and I suggest that maybe we are in for a good stay since we have had our three bad things happen to us. I forget to knock on wood at this time.

We wander around town for a while and eventually decide it is time to visit Kafka's grave. Oddly, the book we have shows his place of work and his home, but does not mention where we can find his decayed remains. There is a young girl in a glass booth in the middle of the square. The sign above her says information, so we assume she is the person most likely able to inform us on this matter.

We show her our map and ask for Kafka's grave. She points to where we are and then to where we need to go. The place where her finger is says cemetery, so we thank her and begin our journey. Half an hour later and we are still walking. The road is alongside the river, which is great the first ten minutes, but as we get further from the heart of the city, it is turning ugly and industrial. Are my feet starting to hurt?

Two months before we left, I decided I needed to get in shape for the trip. I bought this great pair of boots, and every Sunday, hiked up to some waterfalls that are a little way outside of Tucson. The hike totaled almost seven miles both ways, and by the fifth or sixth week, I was making good time getting up there and back. My legs were ready for a trek, and though my feet have always been wimpy and less-than-rugged, they would do fine in my amazing pair of boots.

What I did not foresee, is that we would be walking for ten to twelve hours a day on concrete, asphalt and cobblestones. I have walked my boots to death. Underneath the protective inside of my shoe is a waffle-type base that absorbs and distributes my steps. This waffle-type base is very uncomfortable when it becomes the area your foot is coming directly down upon.

I begin by complaining to Chris that my shoes are killing me, but of course, he has the compassion of a lawn ornament. I push ahead, complaining every eleven feet, when suddenly my pain becomes a limp. Thinking I am cashing in on my fake pain, Chris is even more annoyed with me and pushes on. The underside of my feet feel like they are on fire and I am hoping that I get hit by a car or something heavy falls on me to take my mind off the pain. Finally, we round a bend and see the church up on a hill. Unfortunately, up on a hill means we have to get up there, from down here. I am happy to report that the staircase has never heard such vulgarities, this I can guarantee.

Lush bushes and trees surround the church. The graveyard looks to be a thousand years old. We wander the headstones and poke around the home of the dead. Some of the dates on these stones go back hundreds of years and I get a slight feeling of mortality. We wander here and there, looking, but not finding Mr. Kafka's grave. We hear voices and hold very still as some people walk close to where we are. Now I feel like a grave robber.

I decide to sit down and get my weight off of the waffles from hell in my shoes. Chris continues to poke around and eventually calls me from atop a large stone slab thing, sticking out of the bushes. Atop this slab are four headstones with the name Kafka on them, but none of them belong to Franz. We compare the dates, assuming he may have been buried under a different name, but these Kafkas died years later. We do not even know if they knew him. After searching for a good while longer, we finally give up. I am wondering if this is a joke to play on tourists, sending them to a cemetery that contains *a* Kafka, but not *the* Kafka.

We walk back to town with thoughts of tipping over the ladies little glass booth, but these thoughts soon turn to hunger. Lubos (little bird) told us of a place to eat. He said the food is amazing and the prices are really good. He also said it is a very famous place, and if there is nothing Chris and I like better, it is being able to name drop where we have eaten. The place is called Club Nouveau. I am assuming this is the modern-day name of this place, as its original name most likely forced tourists to sprain their tongues while asking directions to get here.

Club Nouveau is magnificent, and we can only imagine what it was like in its heyday. There are huge chandeliers up and down the room and a fountain on one end. The left wall is covered in mirrors and the right consists of four huge windows, light filtering through paper-thin curtains. The waitress returns to find us staring helplessly at our menus. It is written in Czech, and for all I know, I could be reading mine upside down.

She speaks a little English and we fake the rest. I want a meal that is considered purely Czech and try to explain this to her. She eventually suggests the fourth listing from the top, which, after doing a few animal noises in her direction, I discover I will be having pork. It comes with dumplings and light gravy and I am in heaven. After dinner we order cappuccinos and I declare this to be the best cappuccino I have ever had. To be sure, I order another, and after finishing it, I stand by my convictions.

We then head over to the castle. To get there we cross Charles Bridge. The bridge is about thirty feet wide, covered in cobblestones and has a statue of a saint every twenty feet on either side. One of the statues is of a knight, and legend has it, his sword is buried somewhere within the bridge. As we reach the other side of the bridge, I am excited to see artists, multitudes of them, spreading out their interpretations of Prague for the oncoming tourists to buy.

After climbing many steps, we reach the castle walls. The view of the city is amazing from this height and there are steeples pointing skyward as far as the eye can see. In front of the castle is a group of four men who look like they just came back from a hobo reunion. They are playing some instruments and have gotten the attention of the gathering tourists. This allows us to walk right up to the black, iron gates surrounding the castle's first courtyard.

Suddenly, the changing of the guard begins and we have the best seats in the house. I need to remember to give the musical hobos a tip for this opportunity. After the marching around is over, they reopen the first courtyard and we go in. We wander the castle grounds a bit and I even manage to find a castle bathroom. After doing my business I notice a window that is covered by a wooden shudder. A big yank and the shudder opens. The view is amazing from here and I hurriedly snap some photographs, afraid the bathroom police will wander in and charge me seven dollars for offending them somehow.

Chris has read many things we should see while in here (the castle not the bathroom), but the amount of tourists gets to be unnerving and we decide to go outside for a while. To the side of the castle is a grassy area with a row of trees planted in honor of someone or another. We decide to sit here for a bit and soak up some sun. Suddenly, twelve noon hits.

First a bell goes off across the river, then another. A few seconds later a third and fourth join in. The bell in the church behind us starts to ring and then five more, ten more, twenty more join in. The entire city of Prague is below us and every bell is ringing in the middle of the day. The sound is amazing and deafening, frightening and beautiful. I am listening to all of this and decide this is one of those moments where unusual things occur and I am supposed to make a life-altering decision. I decide that I need to try and amount to something during my lifetime.

To be honest, for a second I thought all the bells would stop ringing at this exact moment, as if I have just made a world-altering decision. But do they? Hell no. They continue to ring for a few seconds more and then slowly die off, one by one. After they all stop, I realize the daylight has never seemed so quiet before.

We go to the main square and look at the tourists. Our backpacks give us away and people approach us with flyers advertising the latest American bar, American dance club or American restaurant. On the way over, I read that over a hundred thousand Americans live in Prague. Everything is so cheap they do not have to worry about jobs, and there are enough of them that they even have their own newspaper. Is that the sound of my brain asking me if this is the place I want to be? Can you imagine how beautiful the city must be after its first snow? Would signing a letter, From Prague with Love, be enough to make me smile every day?

We find a bookstore that sells English language books. Chris feels it is his duty to buy The Unbearable Lightness of Being by Kundera, a Czech-born writer. I cannot find anything I want to buy. We go to a café a few doors down and order some Coke. We write our postcards and stare out at the people walking by. Across the street I notice a Levi's store opening and wonder how long it will take for capitalism to come here full force.

A beautiful woman is walking by our table and I cannot help myself. I grab my camera and take her picture. She turns just as I am clicking away and gives me a scowl. It does not matter though, when I have this picture developed and show everyone exactly what she looks like, they will understand. After finishing our postcards, we decide to find the post office we saw last night.

We are close to the statue at the end of the square and behind him is a building that looks rather majestic. We cross the street and walk up to its entrance. It is the National Museum, and though it is closed, from here we have a straight on view of Prague: the statue, the city, the river and the castle silhouetted against the sky. It is a perfect city.

To my right is an area where they are doing construction. No one is here now, and what has been done so far, is the cobblestones have been ripped up from a thirty-foot area. They are gray cobblestones, no bigger than a coffee mug, and in perfect condition. Has Josef Myslbek, the sculptor, ever walked upon these cobblestones? Did they feel the weight of the oppressive Russian occupied winters? They have to have been underneath the feet of a person who realized that the Czech Republic was free once again. The poet in me wants to have one of these cobblestones. The kleptomaniac in me gets one.

At the post office, there is a wall of phones and we decide to call home. It is weird trying to sum up what we have been doing these last few weeks in just a few minutes, but all they really want to know is that we are not dead, broke or in jail. We then see the sights of Prague, including the old town hall with its astrological clock, watching as death turns the hourglass upside down and the twelve apostles' parade past the windows. Across the courtyard is Týn Church, the most impressive building in my book. Now we are off to find the house of a Mr. Franz Kafka.

Kafka's house is very small and unimpressive and is exactly what one expects. It is at the end of an alley-like street and the tourists push, pull and gather to get in, get out or just be annoying. Chris enjoys the house, but is a little disappointed that they have turned this man's life into a commercial endeavor. He says he understands how I felt at the Van Gogh museum, and then proceeds to buy a coffee mug and a postcard.

After we fight our way out of tourist alley, we head over to the Jewish Cemetery. The cemetery is strange, intriguing and sad. It is a little piece of land that was expected to hold over ten thousand Jews. The headstones are piled against each other, some holding up the others that have fallen. Graves are one on top of the other and give the ground an uneven look. We walk through a roped off section and occasionally see small stones that have been placed upon the headstones, the Jewish sign of respect.

From here, we walk around town a bit more. We see a huge building that looks like a mall, but upon closer inspection, discover it is a K-Mart. These things are bad enough back home, but here? It is huge, at least five floors, covered with everything you would expect a K-Mart to have. I wander around and I eventually get lost. This reminds me of when I use to get lost in K-Mart back home, and then the lady on the intercom would have to announce that if the parents of Vince are in the store, to please come get him.

I have a feeling they would not page Chris though, and if they did, he would not have a clue what they would be saying. Instead, I walk outside of the building and sit amongst the food tents in the courtyard. It seems like forever and Chris has not emerged from the doors. I eat a sausage in hopes of speeding his arrival, but it only accomplishes making me hungry. Finally, I go back inside, and there he is. He is standing next to a bin of pillows, surprised to see me, wondering where the hell I have been. I explain about the memories of childhood and about the sausage and he forgives me.

After a few more blocks of walking around, I tell Chris I feel I need to go home for a bit. I am feeling sick, and it is not the sausage, it has been this way off and on the last couple of days. I think I have overdone it today. We get back to the apartment and hang out on the balcony for a while. The view from up here would be nice if it were not for the two buildings across the way, the three telephone poles and the fact that the balcony faces away from the city. We do have our own bathroom though and this has made all the difference. Chris thinks he sees Boris Yelstin in an apartment across the way.

After hanging out in the one room apartment for a half-hour, I have bored myself and ask Chris if he wants to go back to town. I am feeling better than before, plus I have not been complaining as much as I like to, so I can only see good things in store for us. We walk back to the city and grab a hamburger from a white trailer at the side of the square, which has the word hamburger painted on the side. It is decent in a boring, home-cooked sort of way, but it only cost about sixty cents. We begin to make plans on what to have for dinner.

Toward the river again, and we come across a man photographing a beautiful woman. It looks to be a professional model and photographer as he jumps to different angles, checks the light and talks to her in a nurturing tone. There is a group of tourists that have stopped to watch and they are taking pictures. I can see why they would want to photograph this scene. The man in his zone, the gorgeous Czech model with her face pout and the immensity of the building behind them all come together in a cohesive whole.

I want to take a picture too and am excited to find that I still have some black and white film in my camera. The man tells her to take a break, while he changes his lens, and I approach him. I ask him if it is okay for me to photograph him while he does his work. He looks at me and says, "That would not be a problem at all." He then turns to face the tourists, and in a loud voice says, "And thank you for asking." I take the most wonderful picture. She is sitting on the steps, legs in front of her, head on her knees. He is a foot in front of her focusing on her face. Behind them is an immensely, ornate lamppost.

The sun is getting low and we are hungry. We head over to the restaurant that we had breakfast at because Chris is craving Crepes again. I have a wonderful omelet and then we sit in the Prague twilight, waiting for night to descend.

There are many people selling items from tables wherever we go, and when we take the time to see what they have, we find some very interesting items. Apparently, when the Russians fled, they left behind a lot of their things. It is most tempting as we try on original Russian winter coats, troop helmets, army medals, bear skin hats. The assortment is amazing and the prices are low, but we both wonder if it is a smart thing to wander around Prague wearing a Russian hat, or the rest of Europe for that matter. We decide not to buy these items, though Chris does break down and buy a carved-out walnut with a rubber bug inside, that looks like he is running when you shake it.

After we eat we wander the streets, and in the coming darkness, the city has become very creepy. We walk aimlessly and soon I am lost. Chris is excited because he thinks he has finally found the Prague streets that Kafka always wrote about. He refers to it as Kafka-esque. One road leads to another. An alley ends abruptly while another continues down cobblestone pathways. Eventually Chris admits he is lost and he seems more than happy to say so.

This lost in Prague thing is good, but then the curse of the waffle-shoes starts again, and stepping on cobblestones does not help. I take it upon myself to complain immensely and become pissed that he does not have any intention of finding out where we are. Eventually I am doing the involuntary limp and shower Chris with vulgarities. He is amused that I am not so happy to be lost this time and gives me the shoe is on the other foot speech. He tells me to loosen up, go with the flow and let life happen. Idiot.

If I had any sense of direction I would turn around and leave him here, but I know that he will eventually find his way out if he pokes around long enough, and I will be dead in twenty minutes if I strike out on my own. The walls are twenty to thirty feet above us on either side, so using a landmark to guide us is impossible. I cannot help but wonder if there are bad neighborhoods that we should be steering clear of. I have never heard of a Czech street gang, but I can only imagine what they would do if they do exist, least of all, making us pay them seven dollars for trespassing in their hood.

We turn a corner and suddenly we are in the main square again. Chris has a smirk on his face and I cannot tell if it is pride that he found our way out, or if he knew where we were all along and was just playing with me. Either way it bugs me. Across the river, the castle is lit up with so many spotlights it seems to be glowing in the night. Most of the older buildings are lit up too and the bridge is bathed in light. We head down to the bridge and come across a man playing a violin.

He is wonderful and talented and the sound of the music playing off the cobblestones of the bridge is incredible. He then strikes into a sad version of Memories, which has everyone around him in a trance, and me wishing Chris were of the female persuasion once again. Upon reaching the finale, he bows to the sound of hands clapping and coins piling upon each other within his violin case.

On the middle of the bridge is a group of people our age. They look to be a mix of hippies and backpackers and everyone is sitting around a guy with a guitar. They are singing a Beatles tune. From what we can hear, it sounds like a lot of them are American and the little guy in my head asks me again if this is where I am supposed to be.

After a song or two more, the Czech police come by, two guys in uniforms carrying clubs. They tell the guy with the guitar that it is after the ten o'clock curfew and all music has to stop. There are moans and boos from those gathered, but it is not rude, more like teasing. The guy with the guitar asks if we could just sing one more song and the two policemen smile at each other. They tell him to go ahead. The gatherers cheer the police and the guitarist begins his last serenade of the night. He begins playing Bob Marley's No Woman, No Cry.

After the first few lines, we all join in. A group of thirty people, on a bridge in Prague, at ten o'clock at night, sound surprisingly good to the ear. I nudge Chris and point to the two policemen, they are both singing. Everything's going to be alright, everything's going to be alright…The song ends and we all cheer. The crowd throws tips into the guitar case and two girls jump up to hug the policemen. I find that my eyes are watery. I was not thinking of yesterday or waiting for tomorrow. For just one moment I was in the now. There is nowhere else in the world I would rather be than this place, at this time.

The next morning we see the sights until it is time for our train to leave. We are both impressed with the city, but have had too many idiots to contend with to make the people score high marks. I tell Chris it is the greatest city with some of the shittiest people. He agrees wholeheartedly. If there is anywhere I can choose to live, I am sure it will be Prague. If there is anywhere I can choose to die, I think that will be Prague too.

We board the trains that will over-night us to Munich. As we found out before, we have to buy an extra ticket to get from here to the border, but this one only costs four dollars instead of seven. Either we got ripped off before or they do not charge you as much to leave.

We fall asleep, or whatever it is you call it when you nod on and off on a moving train. The early morning hours let a nice stream of light into our window and I wake up to a beautiful German countryside. We make a short stop at a station and Chris turns to me and says, Shit! According to him, we must have missed a connection somewhere, and are now on our way to Cologne. I ask him if this is good and he says no. We hop off the train at the next stop and get on one going the other direction. We are both sure this will be funny, years from now, but right now I feel like crap and my breath is atrocious. I am sure Chris is no better.

CHAPTER ELEVEN

Bavaria Revisited

Guns, Gummy Bears and Huge Pretzels

We arrive at the Termond's house four hours later than planned. We found out that it is possible to catch a train from Kempten to Waltenhofen, but it only leaves once a day. We are on it and have been deposited about a half-mile from their house. It is raining on us and we are tired. We are going to take at least a day to rest and clean up.

Christa makes us Goulash, the perfect rainy-day meal. She tells us about her father, who had been in the German army during the war. She said he was fighting the Russians when the war ended, and when he got back home, he found out what had happened back in Germany. She said many of the soldiers had no idea what was going on back in the concentration camps during the war. After finding out what his country had done, he changed his citizenship. We have been considering going to Dachau. She says that perhaps we should.

The Goulash has done its job of making me sleepy but the after-dinner drink has not been served. Tonight we have a small, metal cup, in the shape of a wineglass. It is filled with something that will be lit on fire before it is consumed. Mine is ignited first, and I wait for Bart to light everyone else's, which is not a good idea when you are dealing with flames and metal. By the time we blow out our drinks and consume the nectar, my metal rim is hot as hell and I burn my lips. I think Chris has the same thing happen to him. Chalk one up for the Americans.

Bart tells us that he is slowly having car parts shipped in from America. He is building a 1959 Chevy Pickup in his garage, and has only a few more pieces to go. It has been years in the making and he is excited to get it on the road. I mention that it seems the roads are a bit smaller here, and a 1959 Chevy anything is a huge vehicle. He has thought of that, but a dream is a dream and he is not to be deterred.

After a while I am feeling more than tired and think it is time I go lie down. By the time I get into my pajamas, and tuck myself in, I can feel my forehead burning up. Leave it to me to contract some type of Malaria or Bavarian Pestilence on my first real outing. I am almost asleep when Christa comes in the room. She is carrying a bottle and a shot-glass, smiles at me and tells me this is her grandmother's type of medicine. I am assuming it is some form of whiskey by the way my face contorts after my first shot. She has me shoot another one and then tucks me in.

Sometime during the night, I wake up. It is raining and I can see it pattering against the skylight above the bed. Chris is asleep next to me and I can hear the river flowing softly in the background. I am soaked with sweat but feel fine. I must have broke whatever fever or malaria I was suffering from. I drift off to a dreamless slumber.

The next morning I feel fine. I have my morning Coke with toast and we spend the rest of the day eating, sleeping and reading. Chris starts to watch a soap opera with Christa and is mesmerized by the similarities it has to American soaps. After it ends he finds out it is actually an American soap opera, overdubbed in German. He says that explains why one of the characters was named Beth Logan. We put in a video and find ourselves watching Terminator 2. For anyone who has seen this movie, Arnold comes off much scarier when he is speaking German. The cool thing is, his mouth moves so weird anyway, you cannot even tell it is overdubbed. New Jack City, replaces the last few seconds of the movie, and we laugh as we watch Wesley Snipes talking with a German tongue.

I sit on the porch and sketch their backyard, while Chris writes in his journal about our last few days in Prague. Soon, dinner is served and we find ourselves eating a hearty Christa meal. It is a wonderful mess of noodles and cheese and is called Kaesspaetzle. It is gooey, cheesy and delicious and she says the translation will most likely be easier for us to pronounce, Cheese Noodles. An appropriate name I must say.

I down a few beers with dinner and then an after dinner shot. Bart says this is good, because of all the cheese we have just eaten. These will help with the digestion process. That is exactly my intention as I grab for another bottle. While we are basking in our after-dinner glows, Tanja's friend drops by to pick her up.

They are headed to a party for a girl that is leaving for America soon. She asks us if we want to go. She thinks it will be great to bring along two, real-life Americans. We say sure and run upstairs to pretty ourselves up. Being that neither of us will ever make it to the Olympics, this is most likely the only opportunity we will have to represent our country. We want to look good.

Tanja drives us through the Bavarian countryside on a road that is only big enough for one car. Luckily, it is pitch black and she is taking the corners at a maddening speed. I am willing to bet her mother showed her how to drive. We arrive in a small town and park in front of a two-story building. Walking inside, we find ourselves in a woodworking shop, lumber and saws everywhere. We can hear laughing and music upstairs.

There are about twenty people inside a small room at the top of the stairs. Two tables cover one side and crates of beer are stacked against the wall. The host greets us, and since she is the one moving to America, she is appropriately dressed as the Statue of Liberty. Other people are wearing costumes too, including a man with a Hawaiian shirt, a woman dressed as a cowboy and at least three guys decked out as gangsters. Tanja introduces us as the two Americans and we wave like idiots.

The host brings us each a beer and I discover the beautiful nectar called Hefeweizen. Chris is excited that there are buckets of Gummy Bears and he shovels them in by the handful. The host shows us that she has gone all out to make it an American party. Along the wall is a table of food, all the fixings for hamburgers. That is not all, she says loudly, we have all come to a party as true Americans. From under her robe, she pulls out a plastic handgun. I look around and at least half the people are brandishing plastic guns or plastic knives. It is funny, but really sad the way other countries see us sometimes.

She asks me if I can show them how a hamburger is made. She says that she got all the ingredients from a recipe, but does not know what goes where. I slap some mayonnaise and mustard on a bun, plop down the meat, cover with cheese, ketchup, lettuce, pickles and onions, smash it together and dig in. There is a collective, ugh, from the crowd, and then each of them takes turns making an American hamburger.

A little kid sits next to me and we start to talk. Actually, I start to talk, he just holds up different items for my inspection. A woman comes and sits next to him, I assume it is his mom, but I am wrapped up in a conversation with the little guy at this moment. He spills his cup of sticky juice and I get up to find some napkins. When I get back to the table the woman takes them from me and says thank you. I look at her for the first time and her face is a beautiful mixture of Ingrid Bergman and Katarina Witt. I sit back down with a thump. She is tall, with dark brown hair pulled back in a ponytail and big brown eyes. She must be at least ten years my senior. I say, "You are welcome." She looks up at me. "You are American?"

I tell her I am and that she speaks English very well. She says that when she was younger she went to America and hitchhiked in California and all over the Midwest. I tell her I am from Arizona and she says she spent some time in Scottsdale. There goes that damn small world-thing again.

We talk for a while and I am smitten. It doesn't help that I am drinking beer as if prohibition were on the horizon and my only distraction, Chris, is sitting in the corner committing suicide by Gummy Bear inhalation. After a few minutes the little boy jumps from his seat and runs to the door, into the arms of a man that I can only assume is his father.

He comes over to the woman and she introduces us. As a big, dumb male, I automatically do not want to like him, but he is such a nice guy and he looks just like Aidan Quinn. He talks to me for a while about my trip and then goes off to find some food. By this time, the woman and the boy are on the other side of the room. He is trying to wrestle away from her. When she lets him go he runs to me. I pick him up, turn him around and send him back to her. He runs back and forth like this forever, and we are all laughing as he slips and slides on the sawdust floor.

At one point, the kid stops to play with something he has found in the sawdust and I look up at her. She is staring at me and I catch my breath. I will myself not to look away. We stare at each other somewhere between fifteen seconds and fifteen years. Einstein was right when he said time is relevant. I'm having one of *those* moments. One of us eventually looks away. My stomach is queasy and I have a weird lump in my throat. I also realize I have forgotten to breathe. I turn around in my seat and finish off the rest of my beer.

The rest of the party is uneventful, as everyone becomes more and more intoxicated. Eventually, I see the woman putting on her coat and the man is getting the little guy into his. She walks over to me and puts her hand on my shoulder. I feel like Dustin Hoffman in The Graduate. The party has reached an all time high and the noise is deafening. She leans down to me and places her cheek against the side of my head. Her lips are directly above my ear. She says, "Good luck on your trip and have a good time." I lean up toward her, so that she can hear me. "It was nice meeting you." Her hand squeezes my shoulder and I can smell her hair. I want to ask her name, but it feels like it would ruin the moment. As she walks away, her husband and son both turn around and wave goodbye to me.

On the way back home Chris is moaning in the back seat. He says the mixture of warm beer and Gummy Bears is not being cohesive in his stomach. He has a theory. He thinks the mixture of items that he drank have caused the Gummy Bears to congeal into one giant bear, than the yeast from the beer he drank is causing this giant bear to rise up and it is now trying to punch its way out of his stomach.

Due to the giant bear in his stomach, Chris goes to bed as soon as we get home. Tanja and I stay up for a while talking about our favorite movies. I try to get the name of the woman with the child, but she does not remember seeing her and no one she knows fits that description. I know it is a stupid thing to do, but at this age, I like to torture myself whenever the opportunity arises. She eventually goes to bed and I sit in the living room writing down the events of the evening. I consider my first American party to be a big success, even if I did forget to pack a side arm.

I wake up in a strange mood. I plop in front of the television, but European MTV does not hold my attention for long. Flipping channels, I find a news channel in English. I can only assume it is somehow affiliated with CNN. They are doing a recap of significant things that have happened over the last ten years. They show Nelson Mandela becoming president of South Africa, the disbanding of the USSR, peace talks in Israel and the Berlin Wall coming down. It all seems incredible to me. I would not have thought any of these possible and take this as a good omen. Then I sense something strange. Something unusual and foreign is emitting from my person. Oh God, I am being an optimist!

I leave the house and go for a walk. The town is small and I can see a church over the next hill. I head for it, but not before having a conversation with the cows first. The littlest one appreciates my mooing. The other two look at me like I am crazy and continue chewing.

The church is small but elaborate. The main altar is all marble and the front and sides are layered in gold. The walls are covered with paintings, carvings and stain-glass windows. Oddly, the benches for the people to sit are made of wood that is uncomfortable beyond description. This reminds me of what Christa said, about how in Rome, she found it odd that the Vatican is so elaborate and yet outside are hundreds of the poorest, smelliest people she has ever seen. She thought the goal of the church was to help people. Seeing this elaborate church with its uncomfortable benches, I cannot help but wonder if it is more important to build things for your God, or take care of his people.

Deep thoughts aside, I decide to walk along the riverbank. I have to keep moving aside to let bikers get by, which not only ruins my getting closer to nature thing, but also makes me wonder why the hell everyone does not just buy a car. I know I am being an awful American, but listening to the bells asking me to move over every two seconds, is putting me on edge. Then I remember it is Sunday. These people are enjoying their Sunday off. Europeans actually enjoy a real day off during a seven-day week. I am sure the influx of American retailers is slowly screwing that up too, but for now it is fun to pretend. I bet a lot of Americans would love a real day off to become a tradition back home.

I decide to get away from the bicycle maniacs and play near the water. I should know by now that I do not have the ability to tell the difference between a safe distance and too damn close. I walk up to the edge, which is covered with a cluster of little trees. Pushing the trees aside, I plan on watching the water play over some rocks, but instead I find myself pitching forward toward the water.

The little trees are actually no bigger than branches, but my grip on a group of them is enough to keep all but one foot out of the water. The branches bend in a threatening manner as I try to push myself up with the foot that is submerged. The water is cold and I have all but lost feeling in my foot.

I can just picture my body washing up two or three towns away, and my mother asking, why the hell was he playing in a river? This gives me the extra boost I need and I pull myself up. I have no problem with dying, but dying due to my stupidity would really piss me off. Of course the water is not more than two feet deep, but I would find a way to get my head caught between rocks or break my neck or something else poetically ignorant.

When I return to the homestead, I find that Chris and Tanja have left on a hike. Christa tells me that they were looking all over for me, but eventually gave up and left. Brian comes in and asks me if I want to go bike riding with him and a friend. It sounds like fun, but with the kind of shape he is in, I would be lucky if I could keep him in sight much less keep up with him. I tell him no thank you, than I grab a Coke and sit on the big chair at the end of the hall. Reading Graham Greene's Travels with My Aunt, I remember it is my friend Sheryl's birthday. I hold my Coke aloft and wish her a happy day.

Chris returns and tells me that they went on a hike with two of Tanja's friends. They drove up a hill and then hiked from there to get to the peak. From this point, they could see the Alps. Chris said the view was not as good as one would think due to the giant trees in the way, but there was a big stone bench there that he was able to dangle his feet from. They then hiked down to a restaurant and he played the good American by ordering fries and a Coke.

Later, Chris and Christa disappear for a couple of hours. Chris returns fifteen pounds lighter. Christa has shaved off his beard. Years ago, when Chris's dad had been here, she had shaved off his beard. She felt that she should give the same treatment to his son. Chris grows hair rather easily, and lately, his beard had started to take on a Grizzly Adams look. It is not that it is unkempt, just big, hairy and, well, unkempt.

With it all gone he looks like a little boy and does not like all the attention he is getting. I am wondering where all the hair went, but cannot bring myself to ask. She asks me if I would like a haircut and I decline, but tell her I have been thinking about it. It is down almost to my neck and Chris is getting tired of me having to hold it out of my face to talk to him. She tells me she can set me an appointment in town to get it done. I tell her to go for it.

We watch Hot Shots on television, and though Christa says it is a stupid movie, Chris, Bart and I find it hilarious. Chris says it is like the Three Stooges movies, where most women are incapable of understanding why a slap in the face and a poke in the eye are funny. I think most women just have more compassion when it comes to seeing someone have a phalange jabbed into their cornea. I however, think it is wonderful fun, unless it is my cornea being thus violated by aforementioned phalange. Tomorrow we are planning on going to Neuschwanstein Castle, a major tourist attraction and former home to mad King Ludwig II.

We are wondering how to get to this castle, as the trains do not seem to stop anywhere near it. We are thinking of asking Tanja to drive us, but to force someone to go somewhere that tourists congregate just seems cruel. Brian tells us to take his car, we laugh, but he is not kidding. Chris points out that neither of us has driven in Europe, to which he tells us it is no problem. We talk about it and I tell Chris that since they are friends of his family, he will be the one that will be doing all the driving. We come to the conclusion that if the guy who owns the car is willing to take the risk, so are we. Chris is wondering if Brian is naïve or just very, very nice.

We make our way out of the town and eventually find the Autobahn. Chris drives rather smartly, as smart as one can in a Volkswagen Polo. We are amazed at the speeds some of the cars are passing us at. Chris says that he is not going too fast because it is not his car and it is not his time to die.

We arrive in one piece and have a dandy time finding parking amongst all the cars, campers and tourists buses. The castle is unbelievable as we approach it from the road. It sits majestically atop a hill and looks like it is directly out of a fairy tale. When we get closer, we begin to realize how big it really is. The architecture and colors make it beautiful to the point that it looks almost plastic. We have to park at the bottom and walk up the paved trail to the entrance. The courtyard is big, square and filled with as many tourists as can squeeze in. The line is endlessly wrapping back and forth, and not one person appears to have moved since last October.

Our normal routine has been to run from signs of over-tourism, but we have come all this way, driven on the Autobahn and hiked a hill. We decide we will wait in line to see what exactly this mad King Ludwig was so mad about. Three months later we arrive at the entrance. The tours are offered in German, French and English. We pick the English, thinking this is a rather good choice, considering we do not speak German or French. The joke, however, is on us. The woman giving the tour has such a thick German accent, we only understand every seventeenth word. I would be no more confused if we had taken a sign language tour.

The castle is strange. Though it looks huge from the outside, the inside is oddly small. The walls are tight, the ceilings are low and the room sizes are nothing to write home about. According to scholars, King Ludwig spent the country's money building this thing. His bedroom alone took more than four years to complete. At least, I think that is what she said. The way our guide talks, she could be telling us her mother's recipe for potato cakes.

I tell Chris I am disappointed with the castle. I expected it to be full of huge stones, no windows and we would get to carry torches around. I am not sure what he means when he rolls his eyes at me. Chris likes the castle. He does not like the fact that our guide is speaking a weird language, and says the acoustics of the castle do not help, but overall the place is as ornate and tacky as he expects a castle to be. The only thing he does not like is that it takes fourteen hours to get in here, and than we are done in twenty minutes. He says the ratio is a bit off. Now I am sure this place is a subsidiary of Disneyland.

On the way out, we see a sign with a picture of a bridge on it. We assume this means there is a bridge in this direction and follow the path without question. I am thinking that there should have been a sign like this in Amsterdam, pointing the way to the Red-Light District. It could be a picture of a woman's silhouette or two people copulating. Oh wait, that would be much too vulgar and to the point.

The trail climbs a hill and wraps around a small mountain. We cannot really see where we are at this point, as the forest is thick on either side of us. Up ahead, we see Marienbrücke, a bridge with few people on it. Stepping on the bridge and looking to our left, we see the most beautiful sight. The castle stands before us, in its full glory, with the Bavarian landscape as its backdrop. We can see where the castle is built into the hill and the angle is perfect in hiding any trace of bobbing tourist heads. I think I take enough pictures to be able to reconstruct my own castle back home. After a while we scurry back to the castle, to see what the bridge looks like from its angle.

On our way out, we decide we are hungry. Halfway down the hill are a restaurant and a man selling pretzels. We decide to eat real food and sit outside the restaurant. We order Bratwurst and French fries and Coca-Cola with lemon in it. The sun is out and I am starting to feel crappy sitting beneath it. My hair keeps falling in my face and my Bratwurst tastes funny. Somehow, I have fallen into a complaining mode and I did not even see it coming.

After our meal we walk by the pretzel guy and are amazed at what he is selling. It is not that they are soft pretzels, warm pretzels or salted pretzels. It is the fact that each one is as big as our heads. These things are huge! Of course, we have to have a huge pretzel, not only to tell people we ate them, but also to take photographs with. We find a path to wander and kick pinecones as we munch on our twisted, Bavarian treats.

We take a wonderful photo of the both of us munching away happily. I am under the impression that we are trying to eat the whole thing, so I force mine in, even after I would rather not have anymore. Chris is under no such impression and barely makes it halfway. Now I have pretzel breath and feel really gross. Of course, this is no one's fault but my own.

On the drive back, Chris tells me he is excited to see the Monte Carlo Grand Prix. We did not make definite plans to go there. I tell him the money situation is looking rather dismal to be taking side trips, but he wants to go. He finds it amusing that I am the one worried about the money this time.

The next morning Tanja takes us to the station. We both think she is cool, but cannot tell if she really likes us or is just being polite. For some reason, saying goodbye to her at the station is sad, as if we are planning on not seeing her again. Bart figured out the trains for us and told us which one would take us to Monaco. I am wondering if I brought any clothes nice enough to get me into the casino. Of course, if I did get in, I would have nothing to gamble with any way. Six minutes before we are due to arrive in Zurich the train stops at a station labeled Singen. We did something wrong somewhere and are on our way to Northern Germany.

CHAPTER TWELVE

The French Riviera

Stinky Cheese, Dr. Scholls and Unfriendly ATM's

We are not really lost, just thinking that we most likely will not make our train to Nice on time. We take the train into Basil, but arrive five minutes after the overnight train to Nice has left. The accuracy of the European rails is great unless you are running a little bit late.

Chris is excited to be in Switzerland, which he says looks like a wonderful country if you are rich, but he is mad because it looks like we may not make it in time for the Grand Prix. He pulls out the Eurail guide and tries to figure out a way to the French Riviera. For some reason the trains seem to circle around the coast, but seldom just go straight there. He is becoming frustrated and it is getting late. I finally take a walk to the information window and show the woman where we are trying to go. She punches some numbers into a computer, prints out a piece of paper and tells me we will make it on time if we catch a train leaving in ten minutes.

This is the first time I have actually done something helpful pertaining to our travel. It is strange and weird and I do not really care for it. The printout says we have to change trains at Bern, Geneva and Marseilles, but we should be rolling into Nice early in the morning. I do not tell Chris that the only reason I asked is because I do not want to hear him complain about missing the race, and I am under the assumption that being Swiss and neutral, the people will be friendlier here.

The ride to Bern is uneventful and we find ourselves with time to spare. The station in Bern is by far the coolest looking one I have been in. The trains pull right up to the station, so that when you come out, you are facing the front end or ass end of a train. It makes me feel very elite, to walk out and have my train waiting for me at the doorstep. It is kind of like having my own limousine, except it is really big and I have to share it with a hundred other people.

I decide I need a bathroom and follow the signs. I wander into the little room and find myself staring at a hole in the floor. It is an old French-style commode with two grooves on either side to put your feet in. At this point you would just squat. Every aspect of this device frightens me and I convince myself that I can hold it.

Going to the bathroom on the trains is interesting. Like an airplane, it makes a sucking noise and then all is clear. They make a very strong point about not using the bathrooms once the train begins to enter a station. I find a bathroom at the end of the train with a window facing the tracks. Wadding a ball of toilet paper, I throw it in the toilet and flush. Behind the speeding train, I see a ball of wet toilet paper shoot between the tracks. I can understand why they do not want you to do this too near the stations, but I wonder about the people in the country who see trains go by everyday, shooting out their wastes. Maybe the people in Scotland were not waving at me after all, maybe they were telling me not to poop on their land.

The trip to Marseilles turns into a discussion as Chris realizes one of his friends is getting married in less than nine hours. Something about this is bugging him, and it is not that he is in love with her, but that he knows her well enough to question her actions. I tell him that the reason he is so concerned is because he has spent so much time with her, no one could possibly know her the way he does, and this in turn makes him the best candidate for the job of husband. Of course he doesn't want to get married and most likely not to her, but it still sucks to see someone else take on a job that you know you can do better. My perspective seems to comfort him and besides, he adds, love is never based on smart moves or rational thinking anyway.

We pull into Marseilles at five in the morning and hop on the train to Nice. We should be there in time to get a room, go to Monte Carlo and watch the race. The train is nearly empty and we each take a section of seats to spread out on. As the train pulls out of the station, an old guy sits next to Chris. He says hello to Chris and then begins to tell him his opinion on European travel. Chris gives me a look of distress, but I show little concern as I scrunch into my seat and fall asleep.

The train is slowing down as it arrives in Nice and I wake up to the sound of talking. The train is packed. People are standing in the aisle, while I have managed to spread myself over three seats. I apologize to those around me and move my things onto my lap. I wonder if I have been entertaining these people with either a sleep-induced conversation or melodic snoring.

I look across the aisle and see the old guy is still talking to Chris. Chris is fighting to keep his head up and his eyes are bloodshot. He glares at me and I look away. The old guy is talking quite loud and those around him are smirking and joking about him in French. I catch the last half of his conversation, which has to do with the French not bothering to learn English and the fact that America has had to pull there butt out of everything since Napoleon's reign.

Chris says that the old man shared everything about his life since 1941. He talked about fighting in WWII, Korea and being a pilot for General MacArthur. He said that MacArthur thought the Korean conflict would only last three months, but they all think he was pretty much going senile by then. He told Chris he then worked for NATO, which he called a big joke, but it allowed him to play in every major golf course in the world. He also has a skin problem, and has been in the baths at Lourdes for treatments. Chris says he was not that bad, but he really could have used some sleep. I think he was a perfect example of what Europeans call the ugly American.

We ride the train to Menton, where we have heard there is a very interesting hostel and it is not as expensive as staying in Nice, Cannes or any of the other resort towns. We get off the train with two girls carrying backpacks, and since the only reason one would come to Menton is the hostel, we hook up with them. They have a calling card but have lost the number for the hostel. We have the hostel's number but no calling card. It is exciting when things just seem to work themselves out.

The man at the hostel tells us that it is on a hill and suggests that we take the bus rather than walk. The bus costs ten francs and walking is free, so against his advice, we decide to hoof it. The girls are from South Africa. One of them is short, cute and extremely quiet. At first I think she is having deep thoughts and keeping to herself, but after talking with her, I am convinced she is having no thoughts and keeping to herself. The other girl is outgoing and fun and talks our ears off.

We follow the man's directions, turning right after we pass the bridge, up the hill past the fruit trees, left at the hostel sign and down the alley. Then we come to the steps, millions of steps, no joke. They go straight up the hill and we cannot even see the top of them. Chris says he realized the man said it is two kilometers, but he never mentioned it was all straight up. We stop twice to catch our breath and once to remove a layer of clothing. It takes us almost thirty minutes to reach the top, and the only reason we do it this quickly is because we are with two girls. If it had been just Chris and I, I think we would have set up camp somewhere halfway. Chris thinks we lost weight on this climb, I think I am close to hallucinating.

We pay for a room, abandon our bags and head back down to the train station. The race is starting in a couple of hours and we do not want to miss a minute of it. The train from Menton to Monte Carlo is unbelievably packed, but we manage to squeeze on. I am just glad that the trip is only going to take ten minutes, Chris is happy that everyone has apparently bathed. The ticket checkers do not even bother checking anyone as we stampede off of the train.

We buy sandwiches and Cokes from a woman who is Cote de Azur's version of Dolly Parton. She has big, blonde hair and a bosom that makes us blush. Chris is amazed at the fact that someone can live like that, but I am not listening to him, the Marlboro Girls have just arrived and I need all my strength to gawk and stare. One of them approaches me in her short shorts and tube top, handing me a Marlboro bumper sticker. I make noises that are supposed to be my version of thank you, and then she sashays out of my life.

We walk around town trying to figure out how we are going to watch the race. Every place we attempt is blocked off. They really do not want anyone to watch this event for free. The cheapest seats are on a hill, they cost forty dollars and you have to find a spot, climb to it and try not to tumble to your death. We decide that we need to buy a ticket or the race will soon start without us. Our cash is precious and miniscule and we do not even have enough to pay for a seat on the hill. This is mainly due to the fact that we have not found a hostel that is willing to let us charge a room on our credit cards. Did I mention how inconvenient hostels can be?

We find a bank, and though it is closed, there is an ATM out front. We talk it over and decide that since this is such a once-in-a-lifetime thing, and we have not had a chance to really use our credit cards, we will take out a lot of money and buy good seats. The ATM rejects my card. I wish I know why, but since it only lists the instructions in French, I am left to just accept this rejection.

Chris tries his next and after pushing the buttons it seems to want him to push, a steel door slowly closes over the front of the machine. Chris panics and pounds on the door, but it will not open, and now we are minus one credit card. The ATM has an emergency number pasted to the outside, but we cannot find a phone that will take anything other than a calling card. Chris is beyond a bad mood. I tell him the three things one should not lose in a foreign country is their passport, their innocence and their credit cards. This does not seem to lift his spirits.

We find a phone at the train station, in a bar full of drunk racing fans. Chris calls the number and someone answers, but the connection is bad and he cannot hear what the guy is saying. He hangs up the phone and proceeds to have a panic attack. I become afraid for myself and those near us. I tell him to give me the number and I will try. The guy answers and I speak loudly to him. I am hoping to convey that I am in a noisy place and he too needs to raise his volume, but of course, he only continues to mumble. I tell him what happened and he says that we have to go to the bank in the morning to reclaim the card. Chris is not proud of the way he freaked out and buys me a beer to thank me for my efforts. Of course, we are no closer to seeing the race.

We sit outside the bar with our beers and talk about our options. For some reason, they do not accept credit cards to purchase tickets to the race, which strikes us as very odd. I can try my credit card at another ATM, hoping the metal door incident does not repeat itself, but I would rather not. I can sell my passport or my body, though one I need to continue traveling and the other would hardly bring in enough to pay for our beers. Chris appears to have given up. He does not seem interested in seeing the race anymore. I think he is a little sad that we did not get in, but proud that we made it here on time.

The cars start their engines and the noise is deafening, ricocheting off of the concrete buildings with a sound loud enough to make our pints vibrate. Chris says the noise sounds like a wail of banshees in full splendor. I think it sounds like I am trapped under the hood of a Porsche with engine troubles. The race begins and we leave. Chris says this is irony. I think it is sad.

We wander to the train station but it is empty. The next train is not due to arrive for an hour. We go to the smaller harbor in search of a bathroom. We find a shopping complex, but for some reason, the bathrooms remain hidden from us. Chris sees a video game that lets him sit down and race a car. He races for a while and then comments that this is the closest he will be getting to the race. On the way back to the station, I tell him I am going to buy him an ice cream cone. The thought of ice cream cheers him up, but when he sees the man put a sad, little, marble size ball of ice cream in my cone and then charge me eight francs, he just gets pissed. He decides that not only does he not want any ice cream, he wants to get the hell out of Monte Carlo.

The train finally arrives and we head back to Menton. There is hardly anyone else on board as the rest of the population is watching the race. I wonder if we could have tried harder to get in or found other means to pay for it, but I decide that perhaps it is not meant to be. When we get off the train we decide we are not taking the bus and we are not taking the stairs, instead we are going to walk the road that leads to the hostel. This takes forever, but I think it does us good, we need to walk off what has become our adventure to the Monte Carlo Grand Prix.

After taking a shower, I go out to the balcony. Evening is descending and the view of the Riviera is mesmerizing. From this height I can see the lights below as they curve along the coastline. Far ahead is a mountain that eventually works its way into the sea. Behind that, when the mist thins for a few seconds, I can see the lights of Monaco.

On the balcony is a couple in the far corner talking to an Australian girl. I watch the light fade and their talking is no louder than a neighbor's radio, a low murmur in the background. A really tall girl comes out and sits next to me. She has pigtails, thick glasses and sandals underneath her summer dress. She unwraps a piece of the most awful smelling cheese I have ever encountered and begins to spread it on some bread. The smell is strong enough to make the Australian girl stop talking, turn to see what the smell is and then continue with her conversation. I only hope she did not assume it was somehow emitting from my person.

A French guy, Paul, comes out next and he and I strike up a conversation. He is a postal worker on vacation, and though he can afford hotels, he likes hostels because they give him a chance to meet people. The Australian girl, her name is Toni, joins in and we talk about hostels and traveling. The postman and the tall girl eventually leave and I am left alone with the Australian.

She fascinates me within the first five minutes. She has been traveling for three years and does not know when she will stop. Her visa ran out, and if she goes back to Australia, she has to wait a while before she can leave again. She has spent a year in the States, her jobs ranging from lounge singer to aerobics instructor, and has also been to India, Africa and Morocco. She has been in France the past five months and does not know where she is going next. She pulls out these thin black books, they look like journals for accounting, and she starts to write down the day's events. She says that after she gets one filled, she mails it to her mom for safekeeping. I can only imagine what kind of tales three years of travels would procure.

She misses her mom, but she knows that once she goes back home she will not be leaving for a while. This is a life she does not want to give up just yet. Thinking about all that she has seen and the number of people she has met is overwhelming. She is the most free spirit I have ever met and I cannot decide if I envy her or pity her. Of course, she could give a shit if I pity her, and I think I am leaning towards envy just the same.

Chris uses his psychic ability and is able to tell that I am hungry. We head over to the restaurant that shares the hill with the hostel. It is a dinner-only type of place and specializes in Italian food. The weather is perfect so we sit outside on one of the picnic tables. The setting sun and the strings of light above us bring about an air of calm. The waitress arrives and we decide to order the spaghetti.

I have not had any coffee today and am dying for a cappuccino. No sooner have the words left my lips and the waitress throws a fit. She is appalled that I would want coffee with my meal. "Coffee is for after the meal," she says. "I want to know what you want to drink with your meal." God forbid I get served what I actually want to drink. I order a wine and this makes her happy. Later comes the cappuccino, and though it is good, I think I season it with too much animosity.

We eat fast and return to the hostel. The wine has made me tired and the cappuccino does nothing to counter that. Chris and I are the only ones in our room and we have a nice view of the clothesline outside. We are nodding off to sleep and I am willing to bet money I will talk in my sleep about endless stairs, Dolly Parton and withheld cappuccinos.

The old man that runs the hostel wakens us in his own sweet way. He bangs open our door and yells "BREAKFAST!" Normally this would just piss me off and I would roll over and fall back to sleep, but hearing him walk down the hall, banging and yelling at each door, is like an alarm that won't shut off. I stumble to the bathroom and take a shower. Today we go to rescue Chris's credit card.

Breakfast is covered in the price of the hostel, mainly due to the fact that going up and down the stairs, to eat a morning meal, is out of the question. The set up is like a cafeteria with a bowl of cereal for each of us. I sit next to Toni, the Australian free-spirit, who is decked out in an outfit of purple. Her headband, shirt, spandex shorts and her socks are bright purple. She looks like a grape and I tell her so. She enjoys my honesty and the way I flinch when she flicks milk at me with her spoon.

Next to her is an English lady that begins to tell us that she hopes to one day make it as a singer. Toni is acting interested and I am acting deaf. I glance away from my cereal for a moment and Toni has a smile plastered on her face, but she does manage to roll her eyes at me. I only hope the English lady does not offer to sing us a tune this early in the morning, not if she does not want a bowl of Raisin Bran dumped on her head. The old man informs us that breakfast is over by yelling, "BREAKFAST OVER!"

His vocabulary is limited but to the point. I wonder if he is like this all the time. Chris ate his breakfast early and missed out on the free entertainment. The old guy reminds me of my grouchy grandfather and I am really starting to like him. I wonder if he needs an assistant to help him run the hostel, pour the cereal and shout the facts.

We pack our bags and check out of the hostel. Halfway down the stairs we run into Toni. She ran down to the train station after breakfast and is already on her way back up. She is carrying two big backpacks, is sweaty and still clad in purple. I ask her what these bags are for and she says they are hers. She is traveling with three bags, and likes to leave two of them locked in the train station lockers until she gets settled. The fact that she has carried them up the stairs amazes me, but she reminds me she was an aerobics instructor and shows me her legs. They are beautiful and strong and I give her a grunt of approval.

We tell her we are off and she looks sad, I offer her a piece of candy and this makes her feel better. She asks me if we think we will see each other again, I sarcastically remark that she does not have much of a choice, and follow this with a wink. She punches me in the chest with her arm, smiles and continues on her way up. I assume that means only good things. I bet Chris twenty-five bucks we will run into her again before our trip is over. He says we will not and is happy that he will soon be twenty-five dollars richer. Something tells me he is right.

At the train station, we run into the two South African girls and the tall girl who was eating the smelly cheese. We are all on our way to Monaco, so we go as a group. First, we drop by the bank and retrieve the credit card. We tell the man what happened and he goes to the back room, carrying back a box full of cards. We shuffle through them until we find the one with Chris on it, thank him and vacate the premises. I wonder how many cards need to be lost in this manner before they decide there is a better way of doing things.

We meet up with the girls and follow the road to the upper part of town. It is somewhat separate from the boat docks and casinos, on a hill, but relatively close. We go to the home of Monaco's royal family, the Grimaldis, and I wander the grounds. I have a funny feeling that Princess Stephanie will go for a jog, notice me, invite me inside and possibly ask me to marry her. Surprisingly, this does not happen, so we walk to the main courtyard and watch the changing of the guards instead.

Everyone heads over to the tourist booths and I take the opportunity to sit on the wall that overlooks the boat docks. It is a wonderful subject and I take out my journal to sketch. Two minutes later the tall girl is sitting next to me. Her name is Alfie and she is from Cologne. She tells me that she draws too and shows me her journal. Her pictures are amazing character studies of peoples faces. She also has a sketch of swans that is so beautiful, I doubt the real birds ever looked that breathtaking.

She is traveling around Europe before school starts. She has planned on three months, but she is close to two and ready to call it quits. She says she has met a lot of people, but that it gets to be a little weird sometimes and a bit lonely by herself. Part of me wonders if I should invite her to join us, but it does not feel like it would make her comfortable and I am not sure if I want another person on our trip. I tell her I would never have the guts to travel by myself for that long. She says she hopes I never have to.

After touring Monaco, we jump back on the train. We get off in Nice, but only to lock our backpacks in a locker. The girls are going to stay so we say our good-byes. We continue on to Cannes, and the famous film festival. It is time for us to hobnob with the film industry's elite.

Yesterday my feet were starting to hurt. Today they are killing me. I thought that perhaps they would toughen up after having to walk on the near-crippling waffle boots in Prague, apparently not. Since then, I have been wearing two pairs of socks, and this seems to have solved the problem until today. I downshift into complaining mode and follow Chris into town.

Suddenly, like a beacon in the fog, I see a pharmacy ahead. I hobble in to find relief. I know the woman must speak a little English, but she is deciding to play stupid, causing me to hand gesture that my feet are killing me. A dog could understand the charade I give to this woman. She manages to act like I have confused her even more. Finally, I just grab my foot and say "Ouch!" She raises an eyebrow, points to the corner and says "Dr. Scholls?"

In the corner, an entire rack is devoted to Dr. Scholls foot care needs. I grab a pair of insoles, excited that at least this American item has made it across the water. The price of a pack of insoles comes out to thirteen American dollars. These are the same insoles that sell for a dollar fifty at home, but once again I am in a situation that finds me helpless. I hand over the money, and in very good English, she says, "Thank you very much." The French that live on the Riviera are still French, do not let anyone tell you otherwise.

After padding down my boots I leap ahead to join Chris. There is a shop near the main hall that is selling famous movie star hand imprints. They are on big mud bricks and have been signed by the stars. I immediately see one that I want, it is Gerard Depardieu's and my hands are the same size as his. They are beyond expensive and I poke around to see if they have imprinted a smaller part of his body for a lower price. I would be just as proud to own a concave reproduction of his nose, his earlobe or a mole from his back. I have no luck and we continue on our way.

The people are starting to gather at the entrance of where they do the screenings for the festival. Walking by this spot will be the Cohen Brothers, Isabella Rossellini, Gary Oldman and a ton of others. We consider standing here too, but we have only three hours and the screenings do not start for another five. Common sense prevails and we walk on.

Up ahead is a mime that is doing his best to annoy people. He is getting right behind them to imitate their walk. He is funny for the first five seconds, but when the people turn around and discover him, he takes it upon himself to continue annoying them. One man actually stops, turns around and pushes him away. The crowd jeers at this display of mime abuse, but I cheer, but this is only because I hate mimes. As we pass white-faced fool, I see him fall in step behind me. He is imitating me and it is just too damn funny. I am able to ignore him only because I am daydreaming about all the heavy things I hope will fall on him later.

As we near the beach we see a crowd of people in a commotion. We look to where they are gawking and see a man and woman running to a boat. The man has the young Elvis look and the woman looks like an expensive call girl. With his short hair and sideburns, we wonder if it is one of those guys from that Beverly Hills television show. He finally turns around and it is some European actor we have never seen before. The crowd gets excited and waves to him. Chris and I look at each other and shrug.

A second later we see a woman running down the street towards us. She has blond hair and is wearing a gray, pin-stripe suit. The paparazzi are close behind. She passes us and we stare in disbelief. Kim Basinger has just come within feet of our bodies. She is ten times more stunning in person and I am wondering if I should ever wash again.

Along the boardwalk are posters advertising all the movies in the festival. The air is festive and the sidewalks are crowded. We stop to watch a street performer. He is miming his act, but not in the annoying, white-faced way, more in a silent actor way. He is amazing as he plays a piano, hikes a mountain and does a very emotional piece about a father and his newborn. For his finale, he hangs himself, which actually looks quite real. The crowd applauds and Chris says that though the effect was cool, hanging himself was not.

We go to a café and order pizza. It is more like a small cheese crisp and I am disappointed, Chris reminds me that the huge, gooey, cholesterol-ridden pizza I am used to eating is an American invention. I suppose this means finding a Canadian bacon and Pineapple pizza is out of the question. I pretend that this small pizza is an appetizer and order a Cordon Bleu, one bite and life is good.

On the beach, I want to get a picture of me in the water, but it is cold and rainy today and I have nothing to dry off with. I want to prove I was here, so I take off my shoes, lay down and stick my feet in the sand for a picture. The Riviera looks amazing with the sun setting behind the clouds, an ocean liner in the distance and my two big hairy feet sticking out of the sand.

After not seeing anyone else of fame, it is time to catch our train to Italy. On the way out of Cannes, I need a bathroom. There is a big metal thing in the middle of the intersection and it has a bathroom symbol on it. I go to it and put in my coin, but the door will not open. I kick it a few times and try to get my money back, but it is not cooperating. After I decide to give up, the door swings open, but now I am too afraid. The thought of getting locked in and having to spend a night in a toilet, in the middle of a French intersection, is too much for me to bear.

We stop at Nice, and I find myself eagle-spread over our bags. Chris has headed off in search of a restroom. The French Riviera has been an interesting place. We met a lot of people, were present for two major events and I now know that one does not order coffee with one's meal. I only hope I remember that I still have to go to the bathroom when Chris returns. Oh damn, is that our train?

CHAPTER THIRTEEN

Rome

The Pope, Confession and a Coin Toss

We are on an overnight train to Rome. My light does not work so I am forced to neither read nor write. I would use this time to sleep, but they insist on barging in every half-hour to make sure that we still have the tickets that we had thirty minutes prior. On the plus side, I find that these seats are giving me either a sore neck or a sore ass, so I spend my night flopping around to avoid further spinal injury.

The guy in the compartment with us is from Kansas City. He is a used car salesman, but not in the obnoxious sort of way. He is very intelligent, has curly hair and is what I have always thought Bob Greene would be like if I ever were to meet him. He flew to Europe to see the Grand Prix and then will fly out of Rome tomorrow. Used car sales must be at an all time high in Kansas City this year.

When we arrive in Rome two people with backpacks approach us. They tell us that finding a room is near impossible. They give us the name of a hotel that only charges ninety thousand Lire a night, roughly eighty American dollars. We look at each other with the eyes of two people who have come to terms with the fact that they may be wandering the streets all night. Then a man approaches us, he says he is with tourist information and flashes a badge in front of us, which I guess is supposed to make us trust him. I can imagine flashing a badge around an American airport saying I am with the Federal Tourist Bureau. People would laugh at me and then beat me up, probably stealing my badge in the process.

He tells us that a new hostel has opened and is only charging twenty dollars a night. We follow his directions and we eventually stumble upon it. It is a decent place, with the air of newness about it, except for the fact that the toilets do not work. They assure us that they are being taken care of this afternoon and we decide to trust them. We are directed to a McDonalds two blocks down that will cater to our personal needs.

From here, we decide to walk to the Coliseum. It is big, old and highly impressive. The area surrounding it is filled with colorful people and I spend a good half an hour recording their antics on film. We go into the Coliseum and I hook up with the tail end of a tour group. The guide explains how the area in the center, which seems to be a bunch of little rooms, was actually underneath the main floor and housed the animals, fighters or those soon to die.

She shows a picture of how the navy was sometimes brought to town and hundreds of men would be used to hold a giant tarp over the arena, in case of bad weather. A big part of the Coliseum is closed off and we can only assume this is because it looks like it may be toppling over sometime soon. Other parts are open, but so full of Hawaiian-shirt wearing tourists, the ambiance is somehow diminished. I am thinking that if they let more of the tourists into the areas that look like they could topple any moment, there would soon be less tourists to contend with and interesting stories for the press to cover.

After walking around we sit and try to figure out where to go next. Actually, Chris figures out where to go next, I am watching the man in the kilt and bagpipes set up for a lunchtime concert and a group of teenage girls giggle their way into the monument. Suddenly, we both look at each other with the same thought (it is as if we are sharing the same mind, God forbid). We realize we are sitting in front of one of Europe's most famous structures, and forty minutes after our arrival, it serves as nothing more than a backdrop as we try to plan our next move. Chris says it is because the mystery of the place is gone. I think it has something to do with our generation's inability to concentrate on one thing for very long, whatever that means.

Next, we see the Forum and Chris notices it is in ruins, pun intended. I am thinking that this would be a great place to grab a stone to add to my collection, but by the looks of this place, the slightest movement could bring it down. I decide I will await a less frightening opportunity. By this point, besides the cobblestone from Prague, I have added to my collection rocks from Vienna, Munich, Menton, Nice and Monaco. The bottom of my backpack rattles when I walk and the extra weight is my punishment.

From here, we head to the Piazza Venezia, which our guidebook refers to as the centerpiece of Rome. The structure is immense, imposing and quite frightening, but in an architecturally impressive sort of way. I remember writing something down about this place and search my pockets with gusto. I find it, a piece of paper where I have written the name of a church near here that I need to visit. It is called Santa Maria of Cosmedin, is a few blocks away, and is home to the Mouth of Truth.

The Mouth of Truth is a large round stone with a face carved into it. The mouth is a hole that is said to bite the hand off of anyone who lies. I read once that this is where men would bring their brides-to-be, to make sure they were really the pure creatures they claimed to be. Of course, I am sure that once one girl lied and realized she still had her hand, the rest of the town caught wind of this and the whole scare tactic was out the window. I, however, found the Mouth of Truth quite impressive and menacing.

Chris takes a picture of me with my hand in it and then another with my hand tucked into my sleeve and me screaming in horror. I would have made a terrible bride anyhow. We are amazed that such a famous sight is actually devoid of tourists, but we speak too soon, as a Korean family makes its way into the church. We watch in amusement as they take turns putting their hands into the mouth, screech in fear and then smile for a snapshot. Watching five of them do this is enough of a good time and we realize we would rather not stick around and watch the other thirty seven have their turns.

We decide to grab a sandwich, which turns out to be expensive and boring. I order aqua no gas, which up to this point I have always just called water. It is such a nondescript meal I forget what I have eaten the moment

I finish chewing. The Spanish Steps are next on our list of things to do and we head in that direction.

I am finding myself having to just stop and stare every time we come to a red light. The women of Italy are just so many notches above beautiful and this is definitely a city of fashion. Big, curly, black hair, a pair of Ferragamo shoes and an Armani suit, driving a moped through the streets of Rome. It is enough to bring a tear to a young boy's eye.

I expect to experience the same Spanish Steps that Audrey Hepburn did in Roman Holiday, but the staircase is devoid of flower merchants, there is no pot-bellied man offering me gelato and the world has not turned to black and white. We climb the stairs anyway and find ourselves surrounded by backpackers, lunch eaters and drifters of all denominations. There is a man that offers to write my name on a piece of rice for me. Chris is skeptical, but I look at his work through a microscope and it is legitimate. Unfortunately, it is a tad expensive and I would not know what to do with a piece of rice that had my name on it, except lose it or boil and consume it.

We watch people come and go and I tell Chris this would be a great place to propose to someone. He gives me a worried look and I assure him he is nowhere near the top of the list of people I would like to propose to. If only Audrey Hepburn was here, things would be taking a whole different turn, and if she has some gelato with her, all the better.

We are getting the swing of this Rome thing and decide to hit the Trevi Fountain, or as our book calls it, the Fountain of Trevi. It is late evening and there are way too many tourists milling about. Seeing the fountain is almost impossible and we decide to come back tomorrow, as if the tourists will all have gone by then. We get back to the hostel as it becomes dark and are exhausted at having seen centuries of history in one afternoon. My feet are starting to hurt again and I am near the point of buying new shoes. The double socks are not helping, the thirteen-dollar Dr. Scholls are hardly making a difference and I am just miserable. On the plus side, the toilets are still not fixed.

Our roommates consist of a guy from California, who does not say a word, and a really nice guy from Wisconsin who is seeing the world on his own. I go take a shower and find that I am in my first bathroom-shower. I do not know what the real name for it is, but this thing has a showerhead that faces the toilet, and when I turn it on, everything gets wet. The bathroom floor is slanted to the center, which makes the water drain out of the room, but I cannot help but notice that they should have thought of a better place to hang the toilet paper. Luckily, wet toilet paper will not be noticed near this toilet tonight.

The next morning we decide to check out of this love palace. We have come to the conclusion that being without a toilet is somewhere near sacrilegious. Chris has decided that it is very rude of a place to expect him to hold his water. The place we end up has working toilets and is cheaper to boot. Our nice roommate from Wisconsin shows up not ten minutes later. Apparently, people from Wisconsin also know the value of a working commode.

We go to Vatican City and set our sights toward the Sistine Chapel. The museum that the pope keeps is a spectacle to behold. The collection ranges from the eleventh century to the present and is displayed magnificently. I understand now what Christa was saying about the contrast of the homeless outside this structure and the abundance of riches within.

I decide I have not taken enough pictures and talk Chris into helping me add to my collection. A row of stone heads, with no eyeballs, is sitting upon a shelf. As I put my head between them, rolling my eyes, I magically become an important historical Catholic figure. I growl at the animal statues that surround the larger Egyptian art pieces, but am afraid he clicked the button too soon and now it looks like I am kissing a dog. A woman-of-stone is standing erect and her arm is crooked at a nice angle. Standing next to her, arm in hers, we look like the ideal couple. Though posed, these photographs should make for nice conversation someday.

We finally reach the Sistine Chapel and find it to be breathtaking, crowded and humid. The little room looks to only be able to hold a hundred people, but at least three hundred have managed to cram their way in. The ceiling and walls have just been restored and we can see most everything quite vividly. Near the entrance is the wall containing Michelangelo's Last Judgement. It is amazing what one man was able to accomplish in a lifetime. I am only disappointed that the characters are not all in their original naked form. When Michelangelo had finished the painting, the church hired another painter, to add bits of cloth to the more nude figures. It amazes me that any painter would dare to even come near such a masterpiece with a paintbrush, much less tamper with it.

After weeks of travel, I finally have my first, real disappointment. Michelangelo's Creation of Adam, is directly above us and no bigger than a postage stamp. I realize the room is huge and the painting itself is very large, but when you have seen something so many times during your life, you somewhat expect it to blow you away. I only wish I had brought a pair of binoculars. I suppose I can enjoy its beauty up close a little later on, when I go to the gift shop and look through the post cards.

The number of people is doubling by the minute and a few of the more boisterous museum workers are yelling for everyone to be quiet. Overhead a recording plays a repeated message in different languages. It tells us that this is a sacred place and if we would please keep the noise down to a whisper. It also asks that we not use flash photography in the chapel, which is hard to hear over the constant flickering of camera bulbs.

Every few minutes a large man bellows that we all need to keep quiet. At this point an audible wave of shushing works it way through the room, quiet prevails for one or two seconds, and then the noise resumes its previous volume. The man shouts again and the same pattern follows. He is also telling people not to take flash pictures by yelling "No Flash!"

Something tells me he went to the same university as our breakfast yelling host in Menton. I think the best way to see this place would be as a guest of the pope, guaranteeing that you will have time to see it all and that the devices used to keep you quiet are more, well, quiet. I suppose if you are a guest of the pope it would also mean you have a fairly good chance at getting into heaven, or at least having a good word put in for you.

After we leave the chapel, it starts to rain. We hide under the awning of a restaurant across the street. The waiter looks at us through the doorway and I feel like I am standing on his personal porch. We decide this is a good a time as any and go inside to eat. Chris orders lasagna, which he says, is the best lasagna he has ever had. He adds that at times, he gets the taste of Chef Boyardee's Cheese Ravioli, but not in a bad way. I have the tortellini, which is good enough to bring tears to my eyes, that and the fact that I burned my mouth on the first bite. Caught up in the moment we order a red wine. As we are enjoying its wonderful bouquet, we look at the wine list and decide this is one bottle that will be bringing us that much closer to poverty.

The lady next to me drops her fork and I instinctively bend over to pick it up. A noise and movement to my left cause me to pause and I see the waiter diving for the utensil, new one at the ready. He picks up the old one, places the new at the side of her plate and gives me a scowl of disapproval. The rain is stopped and we decide to leave. As we are at the door, the rain starts again, even stronger than before. The waiter tells us to sit down and wait it out. Even after the fork incident he is being very nice to us, so we decide to take him up on his offer and return to our table. He makes it obvious he does not expect us to order anything, but I see a wonderful opportunity to partake of a cappuccino.

We have been here a while and the rain continues to fall. It is nice to spend an afternoon in an Italian café in the center of Rome, but if we do not get in to see St. Peters today, our chance will be lost. We pay our bill and leave a nice tip, even if we both think he should have suggested a much cheaper wine. We run across to St. Peters and are soaked to the skin.

When we reach the courtyard in front of the church the rain stops. The courtyard is a huge round area called the Piazza San Pietro. The courtyard is surrounded by pillars, upon which stand the figures of popes, saints or someone else of religious importance. As we enter the courtyard we head towards the center, where stands an obelisk, with a cross on top. The center is concave, much like the bathroom floor was, and this has caused the rainwater to gather in a rather deep puddle. We are skirting this puddle when the rain begins again. Everyone runs to the sides of the courtyard to escape further wetness. I start to run for cover and then I realize this is an opportunity I do not want to miss. I stop, turn around, and head back to the obelisk. I am the only person in the middle of the Piazza San Pietro. There are few things more important than feeling you have some things completely to yourself.

We walk into St. Peters and the enormity of it scares me. I read once that this church is big enough to hold at least a hundred regular size churches, but that does not even begin to describe it. The pillars along the sides are thick enough to house a family, and the area from the front doors to the main altar could accommodate a good-size town. The main hall is separated into three sections and these branch off into various other sections, each as big as a cathedral.

Before we walk further in, we see a crowd to our right. They are looking at Michelangelo's Pieta. The piece itself is behind a glass partition, but we are close enough to see the detail, including the chiseled signature along the strap that lies across her bust. I have always been amazed that he carved this while in his early twenties, but seeing it in person, I am amazed someone could make anything this perfect at all. Jesus looks at peace, Mary looks serene, and I am feeling pretty good myself right now.

As we walk further into the church, we notice all the different aspects of the architecture. The stone gives way to gold and the gold blends into the marble. Some of the chapels are simple and barren and some look like a costume jewelry store exploded. As we near the end, there sits the most magnificent thing of all, the Bronze Canopy. It is a huge, Baroque-looking thing, which appears both ugly and magnificent. It reaches toward Michelangelo's famous dome with its four spiraling pillars, forming a marvelous structure.

We wander aimlessly and I find myself in a side chapel. There are quite a few people here, but no one is preaching up ahead, so I decide to see what they are all waiting for. The signs say that today is confession day, and at least twenty languages will be able to participate. The one for English starts in twenty minutes, so I find Chris and tell him I am going to confession. He thinks it is a tourist thing, to say you went to confession in The Vatican, but I assure him that I really do think it is about time I start working on my salvation. Really!

I sit outside the confessional and the little door slides open. Forgive me father, for I have sinned, and it has been three years since my last confession. The holy man behind the screen tells me to say what my sins are. I tell him that I really did not come here to rattle off my sins. I am hoping I can just talk to him about things. I hear a shuffling inside and then he opens the little wooden door. He is in his mid-thirties, with light, curly hair and a Chicago accent. He comes out, sits on the steps and asks me to join him. "You want to talk?" he says. "So let's talk."

We discuss everything pertaining to religion. He asks me if I have upheld the commandments and I say that I most likely have done pretty well, especially if we take into account the ones concerning murder, theft and adultery. He asked if there were any others I have broken, and I tell him I am unaware if I have, but he soon lets me know that I have not been an angel in life.

We talk about going to church, which he considers the most important of all, and the thing I have done least. I tell him I like to go hiking on Sundays, and that the trees, mountains and waterfalls make me feel closer to God than any church ever could. He tells me this is a nice sentiment, but to think of it as someone who eats alone as opposed to someone who joins the family. The meal is just as good to each, but when one shares his meals with others, it is that much richer.

He asks me if I have impure thoughts and I tell him all the time. He says that this is something that needs to be worked on. I ask him if he is saying he does not have impure thoughts, to which he smiles and says that it is hard for everyone, but that we should not give up trying.

We have a wonderful discussion about the world and the entire goings on in our lives. I ask him how he knew he wanted to be a priest and he said it was the only thing that he has ever been sure of. What if you fall in love, I ask, but he says that all things happen for a reason. He says that he lets God guide him one day at a time. As I leave, he asks me if I am going to attend church more. I ask if St. Peter's counts as a month of Sundays, since it is so big. He says it does not work that way. I tell him I will consider it and he tells me, with a smile, to enjoy my hikes.

I go downstairs to the crypts and see the tombs of holy men. When I come back up I see Chris, and we notice that the sun has come out, illuminating the stain-glass windows. Off in another section a chorus begins to sing a hymn. I think I am having a near-holy moment and Chris thinks it is a wonderful soundtrack, making for a better experience. Life, he says, should always have background music.

After St. Peter's, we go to the four rivers fountain. Neither of us thinks much of it. I think we are expecting something more spectacular, then again, most things would pale after Vatican City. The Pantheon has been around for over two thousand years, but of course, it is closed on the day we visit.

Chris finds a bit of excitement as he has me take his picture in front of the massive, bronze doors.

We return to the Trevi Fountain and this time it is less crowded. The fountain is an oval pool, with Triton standing over it, guiding his two marine horses. Surrounding this sculpture is white, marble rocks, which look like they were placed haphazardly, but form an intricate maze of fountains. The rumor is, if you face away from the fountain and throw a coin over your shoulder, and it goes in, you will one-day return to Rome. I throw and my coin splashes in. Chris throws his and we hear no splash. I panic and tell him to go again to ensure he will return to Rome in the future. He tells me it is no big deal. He is not that crazy about coming back here anyway. Off to the right is a man selling gelato and I make a beeline for him.

We have found that the people of Rome are the worst drivers in the world. I know some can argue the French are bad, or even the Spanish, but no one can so badly drive a vehicle as well as the Italians do. We are simply trying to cross the street, but the speed at which the cars come around the corner makes it impossible. We walk for at least a half-mile before we get to a spot where we can cross safely or at least with enough time to say a quick prayer. Two lanes turn into five and then back to two. Stoplights are obeyed with lax and stop signs are merely suggestions. The little mopeds work their way around buses and Chris says they look like those little fish that swim around a shark.

The horn honking is getting on his nerves too. They are honking to signal a turn, to display anger and to reward a good move. They honk to fend off others, warn of potholes and to celebrate not being deaf. Chris says the use of the horn here is an art form and says they must be able to get a college degree in the fine art of tooting their horns. I am wondering if they will honk before they crash into me, during or after (probably all three). I'm just glad we were able to use the word 'tooting' in a conversation.

Walking near an intersection that seems to have ten roads merging into it, I see an interesting sight. It is a cobblestone in the road, sticking up a good three inches above its neighboring cobblestones, beckoning me to add it to my collection. Chris keeps a look out as I head into the street. Two feet from it, he yells that a car is coming, to which I scramble back to the safety of the sidewalk. Two more attempts and I finally reach the stone. I grab it with both hands and tug. It is a rather large stone and appears to be somewhat stuck. He yells again, I dodge, and then resume my efforts. The second tug moves it a good inch out of its resting place, but now I notice it does in fact appear to go quite deep into the road. I wonder if these cobblestones could be many feet long in an attempt to keep them anchored into the ground. After another dodge and another tug, I give up. I will have to be satisfied with a stone I have picked up earlier.

On the way back to the hotel, I wonder if, by moving that stone an inch higher, I have made the street more dangerous for the mopeds. I consider going back to stomp on it a few times, but then we see a McDonalds and I forget what I was thinking about. We stop to eat, not because we like it, but because we are poor. It is a sad thing, but when you are trying to stretch your last dollar you tend to only let yourself enjoy one meal that represents the country you are in, the rest comes from the golden arches.

I am glad we have been walking so much. With the amount of fast food we have eaten, any other time I would have had a McHeart Attack by now, or at least a McStroke. Chris notices the McDonald's next to the Spanish Steps is more expensive than the one by The Vatican. I wonder if this has something to do with a secret craving the pope has for Chicken McNuggets. Bless these nuggets, for they are divine, and bless the barbecue sauce too. They serve beer but we do not partake. Chris gets a photo in front of the sign and then we go back to the hotel.

We wake up and prepare for Florence. We have been traveling over a month and today is the first day I feel that I am truly exhausted. Riding into a new city everyday, trying to find a place to sleep, carrying all our belongings on our backs, sharing living quarters with strangers and wearing the same few clothes. It is becoming monotonous. We have been lucky that we have had a bed every night (minus the night trains), we have had a shower every morning (minus the night trains), and we have had enough money to survive. Oh yeah, and neither of us is dead yet, that has to count for something. Of course, this is a once-in-a-lifetime experience, but there is something to be said for chauffeurs and room service.

CHAPTER FOURTEEN
Florence
David, Karioki and a Room With a View

The train stops and the sign outside says Firenze, but the station looks somewhat odd. I remember reading that the main station is located in the heart of the city, but this surrounding countryside looks like an Italian version of Deliverance. Two girls with packs ask us if this is where we get off and we shrug in unison. We decide to stay on the train, which turns out to be a good move as we roll into town. I guess naming two stops Firenze is not confusing to anyone but us.

The girls, Gigi and Mary, are Canadian. Mary is cute and sarcastic, a good combination. Chris thinks Gigi is the prettiest girl we have met so far. I argue that the lady from the American party is my favorite, though Gigi does come very close to ousting her. From our conversation, one would think we have been away from female companionship for just a little too long. One would be absolutely right.

Upon entering Florence, we have made no reservations. The girls are staying in a small hotel two blocks form the station and the prices are supposed to be decent. We tag along and the landlady says she can accommodate us. Our room is like a little hallway with a sink, the beds are against the wall, end to end. The first thing out of my mouth is that Chris cannot sleep with his feet near my head, nor his head near my head, which leaves him with little other options. The window is a thick, wooden thing that opens out to a view of Florence rooftops. Chris paraphrases E.M. Forster by saying every young woman should have a room with a view. He is not crazy about our view, but says that since he is not a young woman, he will have to be okay with a not-so-good view.

I, on the other hand, think the view is magnificent. It looks out over the red-tiled roofs of Florence, and in the background, purple hills reaching to the blue, Italian sky. Gigi comes to our room and asks if we would like to do something later. I suggest dinner and she agrees. This excites us, but we have hours before dinner comes about, so we decide to go out onto the streets of Florence.

Our first turn is a bad one and we get lost. We are suppose to be able to use the giant dome in the middle of the city to guide us, but we end up walking through alleys with tall walls and pass right by without seeing it. We somehow end up crossing the river and wandering into some hills. This type of being lost is fun, but after a while it becomes annoying. The fact that we are walking through forestland while we are supposed to be in the city makes us nervous. We find some steps and what looks like a park, which makes us feel better that civilization is close, but still does not help with the fact that my feet are starting to hurt.

Lost and confused, we stumble onto a parking lot and see a statue up ahead. It is a reproduction of Michelangelo's David. He is facing toward the far side of the parking lot, which we find overlooks the entire city of Florence. How we got that far out of the city, I cannot tell, but where it has led us makes it worth every step.

From here, we have a panorama of il Duomo and the bridge, Ponte Vecchio, which spans over the river Arno. I use up an entire roll of film trying to take the perfect picture. We are all alone up here and we wonder if people know about this spot, but we assume they must, as we see one of those telescopes that let you spy on things for a coin or two. We find a trail that takes us back to town and our upcoming dinner dates.

Something must be wrong with Chris today. Maybe he accidentally used my soap or is wearing my socks. I say this because we are lost again. Everything is fine the first few minutes. I mention that I am in the mood to buy a new shirt and we head off in a direction that shirts may be sold. Suddenly, we find ourselves unable to figure out where we are. We stop to ask a woman where the train station is and she points to the left. We go that direction and find that we have reached a train station, only, it is not the one in the middle of town. Still not knowing where we are, I make the mistake of rubbing my eye too vigorously. To my chagrin, I have torn my contact in half.

Tired and half-blind I stumble behind Chris. We decide to follow the railroad tracks back into town. Our logic is that they will eventually lead us to the main station, but we are also wondering if we are going the wrong direction, toward the countryside. After a while the train traffic becomes heavier and we start to see more buildings. We are behind the main station now and our hotel is only two blocks over. For some reason, when I am lost, I have adventures. When Chris is lost, it is just annoying.

We arrive at the hotel an hour after we said we would, but the girls are still waiting for us. They are poor like us and are looking for someplace cheap to eat. Gigi says that she heard the train station has a restaurant that is supposed to be good and cheap, so we go. Chris orders the lasagna and the two girls get French fries, I get this weird thing that I see displayed at the counter. It is a piece of meat full of spices, but not like a meatloaf, more like a hamburger patty. I finish it, and while everyone else is talking, I go back to the counter to find out what I have just eaten.

The cook tells me the name of it and I let him know I really enjoyed it. He tells me to follow him and takes me into the kitchen. He grabs a patty of meat and puts it into a bowl full of tomato juice. He says let it soak for a while and then take it out. After this, he places it on the counter and begins to massage different spices and herbs into it. Once this is done, he pours some of the tomato juice into a hot pan and then drops in the meat, cooking it with the boiling juice. He lets me know the lesson is over with a smile and a wave of the hand. I thank him and leave, taking with me everything about this food item except its name.

We head back to the hotel and the girls tell us that we have to find a place that sells gelato. I tell them I have had it, but they both swear that a gelato outside of Florence is not real gelato. I would hate to tell that to someone from Rome. We walk around and finally find a small store that sells the Italian version of ice cream. I order something that is the color of cream and tastes like raspberry.

We walk out of the shop and Gigi takes a bite of hers. She spits it out and tells us not to eat it. "This," she says, "is not a good gelato." I tell her mine is good, but she says that she does not want us to think this is the way they are supposed to taste. I tell her I will do no such thing as I continue to make mine disappear.

Back at the hotel, there is only one shower. It is a large bathroom that closes with two sliding doors. Gigi is the first to shower and then I go next. When I return to the room, she is sitting on my bed, hair wet and in a robe. I walk in and she says there you are, gets up, says see you later and walks out. With my eyebrows aloft, I give Chris the international smirk that says way to go buddy, but he appears confused. He says that she came in asking where I was, says she will wait for me and then when I get back from my shower, she leaves. Gigi and Mary are supposed to meet up with this Australian guy in front of the Dome later, and want to know if we would like to join them. Of course, we say yes.

The Australian guy's name is Murray, and the first five seconds talking to him, Chris says that he does indeed have a certain Murray-ness to him. He is one of those attractive free spirits that either attracts or repels women. No one has any plans as of yet and I suggest that we go to the parking lot Chris and I discovered earlier, to look over the city at night. On the way up Gigi tells me that she left home last September and will not be back until next August. That is almost a year without seeing her family. She says her parents keep sending her to different schools and money to travel with, almost as if they are trying to keep her from coming home.

We reach the lookout point and find that it is full of tourists and tour buses. Apparently, we did not stumble upon some forgotten viewpoint earlier in the day; it is just that no one else was around. The place is called Piazzale Michelangiolo. After we ooh and ah over the city lights, we go back down and attempt to find a disco that Murray has heard is good. We wander the streets endlessly and are all becoming increasingly annoyed. A guy approaches us with free passes to a disco down the street, so we go. The dance floor is supposed to open at ten, and it is only nine, so we decide to sit in the lounge and wait.

The lounge consists of big round booths facing a large television screen. We have entered a world of Karioki, which is fine, except for the fact that I hate Karioki almost as much as mimes. The DJ hands each of us a microphone, so that the entire table can sing along, and soon we are one of four tables belting out the words to Bryan Adams, The Simple Minds and Prince.

Gigi is leaning into me and I cannot tell if it is a positive toward me, or because she has lost the ability to balance. Chris does not want to join in the singing, but I keep buying him beers and eventually he picks up his microphone. I am not paying attention to what he is doing, but it looks like the DJ is. After making noises, humming and laughing into the mike, Chris gets his taken away. Sometimes I do not know what to do with this boy.

The disco does not open at ten. They tell us they need more people to arrive. By eleven, the music is thumping, but they still think there is not enough people to open the doors. By midnight we have given up on dancing and have given in to Karioki. Many beers help me make this transition.

Murray announces that his hostel has a curfew and he has to leave. Chris, Mary and I say farewell to him. Then we notice that Gigi is getting up. We ask her where she is going and she says that it is time to go because Murray has a curfew. Chris, Mary and I look at each other, trying to figure out at what point any of us became Murray.

We ask Gigi if she is leaving and she says that we can do what we want. We take this as a sign that she wants to be alone with Murray, but he leaves and it is just the four of us. Assuming the dance floor will never open, we decide to call it a night and head back to the hotel. My bed is firm and we have decided to sleep in. I am excited because we have our own room at the end of the hall. I plan on snoring like a crazy man.

The next morning we sleep in, lounge around and generally take our time. We go to the outdoor leather market and shop for trinkets to send back home. Once again, the beauty of the Italian women strikes me, though this time they are not zooming by on mopeds, they are instead zooming by on high-heeled leather boots. The Italian men are all studs, but this only makes me jealous, so I avoid looking at them. The market is fun but crowded. I buy a leather wallet that smells like a new Mercedes and then we work our way to an outdoor café, where we drink cappuccinos and write postcards.

We go to see Michelangelo's David at the Accademia. The map makes it look like it is just down the street, but we walk for many blocks and are beginning to believe we have taken a wrong turn. Then I spot a cigar shop, and outside the door, are hundreds of postcards of David. They have him posing from the right, left, above and below. They have him wearing sunglasses, boxer shorts or a toga. One has a hole in it for a light switch to poke through and I avoid turning it over, afraid to see Made in the USA printed on the backside.

Up the street is the Accademia, but the line is ridiculous and the tickets cost more than our hotel. The people are barely moving and the museum is not open for much longer, so we decide to forego this masterpiece and return to town. I am positive that I will be back in Florence soon, so I do not feel too bad as we walk away from the cities most famous art piece. I can only hope Michelangelo forgives me this choice.

We go to Piazza della Signoria, a square in the middle of town, where we see an exact replica of where David had once stood. I remember reading that this is where it was originally placed. It was brought in a cart at night, and Michelangelo had to sleep next to it, to keep kids from throwing rocks at it. After several nights, they finally reached this spot and it was unloaded. In the morning, the people of Florence had gathered around it. Michelangelo was expecting the worst, as the Florentine's are stern art critics, but the people accepted it with open arms. They were excited to have something that would bring so much pride to their city.

We go inside the building it guards, Santa Croce, and see where some of the cities most elite are laid to rest. Michelangelo's tomb is impressive, adorned with marble figures resting upon it. Dante's tomb has a life-size marble statue of him, looking both frightening and scholarly, though his body is not actually in this location. Galileo takes up a smaller portion of the wall, and a little further down, a plague commemorating Leonardo Di Vinci. Outside is a garden of sculpture, but it is fenced off and we are in no mood for scaling.

From here, we walk to il Duomo and I am mesmerized with all the people. I cannot stop taking pictures of the panhandlers. With their soiled garments and handlebar mustaches, they look like they have been dropped here from another century. The art around il Duomo is impressive, as is the enormity of the dome itself. Every street in Florence has been right out of a picture book and I have gone through almost all of my film today. The rest of the day is spent looking at art, people and buildings. I eventually come to the conclusion that Florence is now my favorite city.

We eat at a restaurant that specializes in my favorite thing, calzones. We then walk off dinner by going to the main bridge to watch the sun set. The wall around the river, as with most of the walls in Florence, is pietra serena, the serene stone of Florence. It is a special stone that comes from the hills around this area and I decide I want some. My rock collecting habit has become obsessive, but it is too late to stop now.

I remember that a friend of mine told me that her dad took a rock from Russia when he was visiting there. They caught him at the airport and told him it was considered stealing from their country. He was let go, oddly enough, with the rock still in his possession. I wonder what the rules are against taking European rocks. Surely, it is not as bad as taking an artifact, painting or the skeleton of a saint, but then again, who knows? I am weighing the pros and cons of this endeavor when I see what I want. A piece of the wall has broken off and shattered on the ground. There is a triangular piece as big as my hand that somehow tells me it has always wanted to see the States. Assuming it will only be swept up and thrown away, I give in to its request.

On the way back to the hotel, we stumble upon an American bookstore. I want to buy something to read but cannot help but feel guilty that I still have not read Don Quixote, so I abstain. The girls have just returned from a day in Pisa. We are all going to Venice tomorrow, but we are leaving early and they are taking a later train. Gigi tells us to meet them in the main square, where they will be meeting Murray, and then we can all ride the Gondolas. We agree and then head to our rooms.

It is raining hard and there is a rainbow outside. The smell of wet is sleep inducing, so we decide to leave the window open. Later, the sound of obnoxious Italian teenagers is not sleep inducing, so the window is closed. Tomorrow we reach Venice, Italy's city of the canals.

CHAPTER FIFTEEN
Venice

Green Gum, a Boat Race and the Oldest Men in the World

The canals of Venice are like the streets of Florence, each one demands a photograph be taken. We arrive midday and sit upon the steps of the train station. Chris says they remind him of the Spanish Steps, with all the people hanging out, except these steps are more horizontal than vertical. I take this opportunity to sit in gum.

It is not only gum, it is bright green gum, fluorescent green to be exact. It is right in the middle of my butt, between my pant pockets, and is as big around as a soda can. I take this opportunity to make a point to Chris. I shrug, survey the damage by walking in circles trying to get a good view of my ass and then untuck my shirt to cover it. The gum would normally make me angry, but I feel like showing Chris how one can act calm in times of crises. Plus, I have bigger fish to fry as my body begins to rapidly deteriorate.

First, I think I may have broken my leg, and it feels like the bone is trying to push its way through my left shoe. I also have a headache that is working its way down my spinal cord. I decide to take some time and figure out what else is wrong with me. My feet are hurting, which is odd after sitting on a train so long, and I can only assume I have developed some type of tumor somewhere. I am also wondering why my nipples seem so sensitive today. I ask Chris if he thinks I am likely to lose one, but he does not offer much in the way of support. I tell him that if I ever did lose a nipple, I would replace it with a gold one. His only contribution is to tell me that I have finally snapped.

After my bout of complaining ends, we tour the town. We both agree that Venice is the most romantic city we have visited. I am thinking it should be called city of the couples, which is all we seem to see around us. I bet some hotels are just one big honeymoon suite. Chris agrees that it is very romantic, which he says is not good being that he only has me at his side. We both agree this is a city we need to return to, but not together, nor alone, if you catch my drift.

We book a room at the hostel and then return to our walk. The shopping district is crowded and the roads are the size of alleyways, but the amount of Venetian glass on display is overwhelming. I go into the first couple of shops, but having to work my wide shoulders around balancing glass makes me nervous. Then I make a mistake of looking at the prices of some of these things and decide window-shopping is more my forté.

I cannot wait any longer and ask if we can go to the main square, Piazza di San Marco, the subject of some of Canaletto's best paintings. The church of San Marco is beautiful with its ceiling of gold and its art-filled walls. Outside, smaller flags of Venice surround a huge Italian flag. They billow in the wind. This, added to the throngs of people and pigeons running about, makes Chris declare this a perfect town square. We watch the kids chase the birds and the parents chase the kids. We are supposed to meet the girls here, and can think of no other place we would rather wait.

The brickwork of the square is intricately designed, with patterns of lighter bricks working their way through the darker ones, giving it an appearance of a maze. The buildings on either side are large and imposing, but arched entryways, supported by stone pillars, result in a more open atmosphere. Above these pillars are smaller ones, separating the windows and above those, even smaller pillars that reach up to the roof. When we first arrived it all looked much bigger, but as evening approaches the cafes that line the square have put up their outside tables, and it is at one of these we plant our weary bodies.

Each café has its own mini-orchestra, which consists of a man at a piano, one with a violin, a cellist and possibly an accordion player. The one we sit at plays Memories, and it takes me back to the night on the Prague bridge and the man with the violin.

A bit later, a group of kids begin to do a conga line. They are hopping about and laughing and more and more people join them. Pretty soon it is at least fifty people long and the entire square makes way as they snake across the stones. Someone tumbles and the line breaks apart. The participants applaud and then disband. To our right, the sun is slowly making its way behind the buildings.

I order an iced tea and Chris has a cappuccino. He says this is the best one he has had so far. He thinks it is funny that he is sitting in a foreign country, looking at ancient churches, having a cappuccino in a piazza, and it all seems perfectly normal. This is what he has been waiting for all his life. I love the fact that Chris can appreciate things the way he does. On the glass-is-half-empty side, he is mad that his pen leaked into his journal and he somehow got a scratch on the face of his watch. I silently sip my iced tea.

As we watch people, Chris says he has never seen so many over-tanned, dyed-blonde, bright lipstick-wearing people in his life. He has also never seen so many older men spending time with their nieces. This is the first time I have felt so underdressed, not excluding the wad of green gum stuck to my ass.

The Italians seem to be very conscious about their appearance. However, not always in a way that makes them look good, but sometimes in a way that makes them look like they have put a lot of time and money into it. I say that they love their shoes and they love their glasses and they really like their hair too. Chris likes this and writes it down. I just love being quoted.

We assume the girls are not coming and ask for our bill. It comes out to seven dollars apiece. I cannot fathom how an ice tea can be as much as a cappuccino, all you do is put leaves in water and then wait. Chris thinks that maybe all the drinks are the same price and I am thinking that they are probably screwing the underdressed tourist with the green gum on his backside. Either way, we pay and leave.

Near the church is a mob of people. We instinctively head over, expecting to see a fight. Instead, we find a church choir welcoming in the night. They belt out a few songs, and we are preparing to leave, when they begin to sing Little Drummer Boy. This is my mom's favorite song and I can only imagine how perfect this all would be for her to experience. The song is not too long, but long enough to make me miss my youth and my mother.

After they finish singing, we walk to our right, which is the main entrance to the square. This spot is where the boats would dock when royalty sailed into town. They would pull up in front of the library and make their way past a lone pillar, the San Teodore Column, entering the San Marco square. These days, just off the pier, there are wooden poles sticking out of the water. These are used to hold the gondolas when they are not being used. To our right and across the water, we can see the great, white domes of the capitol building and if I remember correctly, the Grand Canal begins near there.

We are at the edge of the walk and the lapping of the water causes the gondolas to knock against their wooden posts, a sound that is both eerie and beautiful. The lights on the opposite shore are a soft white and the boatmen's lanterns are a pale yellow. The music from the square drifts in and out, while across the water, we can hear a gondola driver singing softly to his passengers. It is eight-thirty and twilight descends on Venice.

We catch a boat to the hostel, which is not as easy at is sounds. It is much like waiting at a bus stop, but the boats are few and far between, which makes for more people wanting to jump on. I do not really mind being crammed in a boat, but any transportation that carries a slight threat of submersion with it, always makes me leery. We finally reach the hostel and find that we are sharing a room with two of the oldest men in the world. I guess that they must each be close to ninety years young. Chris does not think they are that old, but I was the one that saw them in their underwear.

The walls that separate the rooms are not real walls, only sort-of walls, as they stop two feet short of the ceiling. This would normally not be a problem, but tonight an Italian-youth soccer team is occupying the room next door. They are the loudest people on the face of the earth. At one point, the two old guys make their way to the restroom and I yell at the top of my lungs for everyone to shut up. They are so loud they do not even hear me. The two old guys return, tell us goodnight, and are somehow able to fall to sleep. I wonder if it has to do with a slight loss of hearing or if they have each mastered the art of Zen.

I wake up feeling crabbier than usual, and can hear the young soccer club has finally fallen asleep. The two old guys are gone and we are minus a good night's sleep. Packing our things has never been done as loud as it is this morning. I not only hope we have awakened some of them, I also hope they lose their game today. I can hold a grudge like the best of them.

We go to the Bridge of Sighs, which has something to do with being the last place prisoners crossed before they entered the prison. A gondola is passing underneath and the driver is wearing a black and white striped shirt and a big black hat with a red ribbon around it. I take a picture that will make postcards envious. We have been contemplating a gondola ride, but upon inquiry, we find that the starting price is around sixty dollars for a half-hour. Even if it were less, I think we would have thought twice about snuggling together in a boat careening down canals of Venice. The price keeps us from having to take that route.

Walking over a bridge, I notice a lot of people leaning outside their canal-facing windows. Off in the distance we see boats heading in our direction, we decide to await their arrival. Pretty soon, the entire area fills with people trying to catch a glimpse. The boats reach us and we see that it is a parade of contestants. The Venice boat races are only a few days away.

The parade lasts all morning as hundreds of entries paddle by. We see a miniature Viking boat, manned by muscular, blonde-wig wearing Italians. There is also an entry of a boatload of chefs, one full of court jesters and one that looks like a Chinese dragon boat. A canoe full of nuns rows past, only to be followed shortly by a boat full of monks. Everyone is in costume, the atmosphere is sophomoric, and after we watch a man swim past with a flag on his head, a boat overflowing with vegetables makes the crowd erupt with glee. The oarsmen answer all of our cheers by raising their paddles straight up into the air and shouting back. Today I discover that I want to be a Venetian.

After the parade, we go to Harry's Bar. Chris is excited to see it because Hemingway talks about it so much, but the bar disappoints him and he decides to go in next time. Our friend, hunger, finally catches up to us and we decide that today is a day for a fine Italian meal. We wander away from the tourist area and the boards outside the restaurants that advertise the gastronomically delightful Tourist Menu. Looking at some of the offerings for such meals is not only sad, but also offensive. Feeding people badly seems so unlike a country so proud of its cuisine, but I suppose the day to day question of what one should eat would cause me to put up such a sign too, or eventually stab someone with a fork.

Soon we are lost, then we see a restaurant, two things that go well together. We sit at an outside table and excitedly scan our menus. I have found that Italy is the easiest country for me. The menus are easy to pronounce, even if you do not know what you are ordering, and conversations are easy to have if you just let the other person talk while you shake your head up and down. I have also found that by using my thumb to signify I want one of something, saying things like bella (beautiful), bravissimo (bravo) or Dio Mio (My God!) and mispronouncing words like Coca-Cola, I am being accepted as one of their own.

A simple nod tells the waiter we are ready to order and pointing to the menu tells him what we want. As long as he does not ask us anything difficult, like if we want cheese with that or if we would like to have some water, we will most likely be mistaken for Italians.

We each order the lasagna as our first course. For the second course, Chris goes the way of the fish while I go the way of the chicken. After that, he decides he needs roughage and orders a salad. I decide that the last thing I want is roughage and settle for some tasty frittes. He ends his meal with a fruit bowl and I end mine with a cappuccino. Sometimes I think what people eat can tell you a lot about them. With our meal, we also ordered a bottle of wine, and even though I thought we have each had half, Chris is acting very loopy.

I found out somewhere in Rome that most restaurants do not bring you the check because they feel that is rude. Instead, they wait until you ask for it or you make like you are about to leave. After figuring this out, I both enjoy and am annoyed at watching boisterous Americans become disgruntled as they wait for the check to arrive. It is not their misunderstanding of the way things work that bothers me, it is that tend to become loud and rude during the learning process.

Gigi gave me a patch of a Canadian flag and I have it on my backpack, as a tribute to all the Americans that are allowed to go on vacations. We grab our things, as if to go, and our check magically appears. We pay the man, and after he gives me the change, I stand up. I now know exactly where the other half of that bottle of wine went.

We stagger to the main docks and jump on one of the bigger boats for a ride around the canals. The views into the house-lined canals is inspiring, I only wish I had time to sketch the city for weeks on end. After our ride, we go back to the square and watch the people. There are as many tourists here as anywhere, but when you enter a place as big as this, it always appears empty. I count over a hundred people milling around, though it looks like hardly a few. As evening approaches, we need to start heading toward the train station. Tomorrow we will be returning to Bavaria, and our last visit with the Termonds. That is, of course, if we can survive one more night train.

We are still full from our meal, but Chris is inspired to try and fit in more food. I decide not to let him tackle this endeavor alone. We stop and try a cannoli and then wash it town with a gelato. If I lived in Italy, I would be two hundred pounds heavier, but I would also be two hundred pounds happier, so I guess it all would even out.

CHAPTER SIXTEEN
Dachau
The Past, the Present and a Simple Rock

The train ride from Venice to Munich is providing me with some wonderful examples if I should ever have to answer the question, what is hell like? Our compartment sits six people, which is fine, unless six people actually want to use it. I have to sit up straight, knee to knee, staring at a stranger's head while they stare at mine. There is an English girl on the train with us, which makes it a bit more bearable. She talks a bit loud, but for once, it is someone annoying me in my own language. I am slightly amused.

The way one feels after spending an entire night on a train is much the same as surviving a cross-Atlantic flight. You just want to shave off all your hair, sit in a warm tub and have pretty women scrub you down with toothbrushes. At least, that is what I would enjoy right now. We both nod off and on during the trip, which only makes me crankier than usual as we roll into Munich. I am not a morning person and this fact is starting to get on Chris's nerves. He tells me to just deal with it, which is fairly bad advice to give someone when they are already at a point that they are unable to deal with most anything. Maybe I need some sort of therapy for this problem, then again, maybe I just need people to leave me the hell alone until noon.

We arrive at the Termond's house. They are not home, but they have left us the key in the mailbox. Chris heads to the laundry room and I head to the shower. Afterwards, I gorge myself on items found in the kitchen then drag myself upstairs and fall asleep. Chris washes all of his clothes and then takes a shower. I am not too sure I understand the order he does things in, but I am sure he is probably thinking, you shower, eat then sleep! Are you mad?

When I wake, the family is home. We pitter around for a bit, I do my laundry, then Chris and I decide to go for a bike ride. We only get a mile down the road and it starts to rain on us. We go back and decide to play basketball in the driveway. The hoop is above the door, but lower than a regulation one, so we take turns slam dunking the ball and feeling macho. We go inside and see if we can help Christa with dinner. She has a radio in the kitchen and I hear a Counting Crows song. I take this as a positive sign and it makes me very happy.

Brian has brought his girlfriend over for dinner. She is really nice and speaks wonderful English. We are fed a meal of roast pork, dumplings and red cabbage. I think I really like dumplings now. We have another in-depth discussion about religion, and Christa and Tanja really get into it. Then Chris and Christa discuss patriotism in Germany.

I sit down with my journal and it hits me that we are only a week away from the end of our trip. It seems to have gone by very quickly and has also dragged at times. The whole England/Scotland part seems like it was an entirely different trip and I am having trouble remembering some of the details. This memory malfunction I inherited from my dad. I try to figure out what I have learned or what sort of epiphany I can share with others, but can come up with nothing better than buy thicker socks. I still have a week to go and perhaps it will all come together in my head soon.

It is morning and I have awakened to the sounds of a light rain. Today is the day we visit Dachau. Chris did not wake me up on time and now I have only thirty-five minutes to get ready. We catch the train into town and I am cranky as ever. I find an apple and some Ritz crackers in my backpack, and this helps calm me down a bit. From town, we have to catch a bus that will take us near the camp, and then from there we walk.

The bus is a mix of people and everyone is appropriately quiet for what they are about to experience. Everyone, that is, except the three girls from America. Barbie and her two sorority-sisters talk, laugh and generally look like idiots. Because of their jabbering, we almost miss hearing the driver announce our stop. The loudest of the three is blonde, perky and is wearing what looks like a cheerleading outfit. I only wish I had brought my Canadian patch with me. The bus leaves us off almost six blocks away from the entrance, and we are fortunate to find ourselves walking in front of the girls from the Ima Bigga Ditza Sorority. We distance ourselves as we near the gate.

The entrance is right off the street and from here, we can only see the fence, a large building to our left and a guard tower straight ahead. As we pass the building and come around the corner, we find ourselves standing in the main parade grounds. The ground is covered with gravel and I can only imagine the number of people who engaged death in this area no bigger than a football field.

They use to make them endlessly march here until some fell dead and others were shot. They would have to stand here for hours, in the middle of winter, for no other reason than cruelty. The gray skies above us seem to be a part of the camp setting and I cannot picture any of this bathed in sunlight. I wonder if the sun ever shines here.

Most of the people from the bus head toward the museum, so I decide I am going to walk around the camp first. Chris has already distanced himself from me and I can tell he wants to see it by himself.

First there is the barracks, of which only a replica stands, as the originals were destroyed when the camp was liberated and slowly thereafter. The barracks are said to have housed over ten times the number they were made to. Five or six people occupied each bed and the toilets were in the room next door, of which I only counted eight.

Behind the barracks are rows of cement slabs. They look like concrete lots in a trailer park, but each one represented where a barrack once stood. The number is overwhelming as it stretches the length of the camp, and to think, each one of these was holding up to ten times it allowance. Toward the end of the rows of concrete is a round, brick building with a cross on the front. The plaque says this is the Christian chapel. To the right is another shrine. This one slopes into the ground and has a big Star of David on the gate. It is the Jewish memorial chapel.

I follow the path around and enter a wooded area. There is a tour ahead and I decide to join them. We first come to a clearing that has a low, man-made ridge on one side. It looks like a dirt speed bump. The guide says that this is where they tied people to stakes for target practice. The rise of dirt is for the blood will have somewhere to drain after they are shot. Further down we see another one of these, but this one has been covered over with hundreds of roses. I notice none of them are red and wonder if this is intentional.

Further along we see the gallows, where countless were hung, and a large dirt area with a Star of David in the middle. This is where the ashes of thousands of people were found, all thrown together in one big hole. The guide said that the Germans prison guards would often come here to fill jars with ashes, and then take them to town to sell to the families of prisoners, claiming they were their last remains. The prices were astronomical, but they knew that everyone would pay to have the last remains of a loved one. This went on for years. Across the path is a statue of a camp prisoner. He is bald, his clothes are hanging and his shoes look too big on him, but he is holding his head up high.

We walk along the creek and we see a clearing outside of the gate. That, he tells us, is where they would kill the Russian soldiers. They were shot by the hundreds and no one knows exactly who or how many died this way. No record was kept of these killings. Once in a while, they would take them outside the camp and pretend they were letting them go, but up ahead would be a squad of soldiers waiting for target practice to begin.

I leave the group and walk to the buildings on the right of the parade grounds. The first one is a large hallway with huge doors along its side. I pull open one of the doors and the outside light shows me what looks like a huge closet. There are pipes along the top of the room. These are the gas chambers, though no one was ever gassed here. Next door is a large room that appears to be a shower. The sign says that this was the camp shower, but was also built as a giant gas chamber.

Further, along I come to a room with two men taking pictures. One is snapping a photograph while the other poses with his foot up on a large brick object. He sees me and hurriedly steps back over the Do Not Cross chain that is strung along the front. After they leave, I notice why he looked so guilty. He had been posing with his leg on top of an oven, the same ovens that were used to cremate tens of thousands of Jews. I hate tourists.

I head across to the barracks, to take one more look inside, and then walk to the museum. As I round the corner, I see Chris. Something makes me stay where I am so he does not see me. There is a stone wall, with the words Never Again displayed in five languages. In front of this wall is a square stone, about two feet tall, with a metal lid on top. Inscribed on the side of the stone is Ashes of the Unknown Concentration Camp Prisoner. On top is where people have left their stones, a part of the Jewish tradition, as a sign of love and respect. I watch as Chris looks around the empty parade ground, picks up a rock and places it on the stone. I decide not to tell him I see him do this, but am glad just the same.

I come around the corner and we go into the museum. The first thing we see is a map of Europe. Each place that had a camp is shown with a red dot. The number of red dots is unbelievable. There must be hundreds. From the red dots, there are arrows, which show the routes prisoners were taken from one camp to another. It explains how far Germans who opposed the government went, how far enemies of war were sent, and then it shows how far the Jews were sent. In the middle of the map is a red dot for Aushwitz, the final destination, and next place you would be sent if you survived Dachau.

Beyond the map are wooden pillars from floor to ceiling. Each one has a black band around it and a countries name printed on it. I think it was showing how many countries were victims of this genocide. The entire room is filled with pillars and we have to find our way through it like a maze, in order to reach the next room.

Along the main room are huge blow-ups of photographs depicting camp life. The first few pictures show Jewish children being led out of the Ghetto by gunpoint. Then we see men and women behind barbed-wire fences, a beautiful woman who has just arrived to the camp and an older gentleman that looks more skeletal than human. Toward the end, the pictures depict various scenes of torture used on the prisoners and we see a woman and her three children being led to the furnaces.

The last picture is of a ghetto. It is almost a beautiful photograph if not for its content. It was taken in the early morning, the sky is fading into light and the fog is still hanging low to the ground. The buildings are nothing more than silhouettes and the streets are completely empty. Below the picture is only one sentence. The Answer to The Question of the Jews.

There is a film that they are showing and we crowd into the theatre with the others. It shows camp life as the Germans filmed it and then what camp life really was like. The look on these people's faces is beyond description. We see the Allied Forces liberate the camp and cheers of joy and tears of relief as they realize their nightmare is over.

They explain that most of the town's people were told it was a meat factory for the war effort, which explained the smoke and the smell. Even top city officials did not know what went on behind the gates. We see them tour the camp after its liberation, a film crew following. They open a door and the camera focuses on hundreds of bodies piled atop one another. The Germans had run out of coal before the Allies arrived and were not able to burn them fast enough. One man turns himself away and the woman behind him has an unobstructed view of the room. The look of horror on her face says it all.

During the movie, the audience is completely quiet, with only the occasional sound of someone crying or gasping. After the liberation of the camp, they show the prisoners that were left, walking out the front gate and onto the road. Now they begin their long walks home, to see if any of their loved ones survived. We can hear the sounds of their footsteps scraping against the paved road. Then very softly, we hear a man's voice, he says do not ever forget what you are seeing here, ever.

The lights go up and no one is moving. I am just leaning over and sobbing. No one knows for sure how many people were here, but the Germans records show over 200,000 prisoners. Of these, 30,000 people died in this camp during the twelve years that it was open. Our group shuffles out of the theatre and toward the doors. Beside the exit of the museum is a sign, a famous quote, from Santayana.

Die sich des Vergangenen nicht erinnern, sind dazu verurteilt, es noch einmal zu erleben.

Those who cannot remember the past, are condemned to repeat it.

We leave the museum and everything looks different. It looks less like a historical monument and more like a cemetery. Every corner of this place is where someone died or watched a loved one die. Then I remember something that the tour guide had told his group earlier. Despite the hardships, the bloodshed and the hopelessness, there is not one recorded case of a prisoner having taken his or her own life. I pick up a rock and place it on the square stone next to the wall, out of love and respect.

We go back to the Termond's and Christa asks me what I thought of the camp. I tell her I really cannot put any of it into words, in fact, I almost feel like I should not be able to. She tells me she understands and had the exact same reaction when she went. She says she sometimes hates recommending people go there, but feels it is only right that people see what humans are capable of. Chris has not said a word about it and I can tell he probably will not. I feel like we have just been to a funeral for a friend who has died needlessly. It leaves me feeling helpless and sad.

CHAPTER SEVENTEEN

Kempten
One-Way Streets and a Girl Named Mona

During dinner, Christa tells me that she has made an appointment for me to get a haircut in town. The place is called Boblines, and is one of the best in Kempten, but I am not so sure I can afford the best in Kempten right now. She calls back and their prices are a little steep for my budget, but then they recommend that I let the apprentice cut my hair for a much lower rate, and I agree.

I spend the evening sitting on the back porch. As the end of our trip draws near, I am becoming more appreciative of my surroundings and more depressing in my thoughts. After tomorrow, we take the train to Paris, the last city on our European tour. I feel like waxing nostalgic over a trip that is almost over, but right now I have more important things to attend to, like figuring out how to get a big wad of green gum off my pants.

The next morning we take Brian's car into Kempten. Chris has become cocky with this whole driving in Europe thing, though he admittedly does not quite understand what all the signs mean. We both figure that as long as we know when to stop and when to go we will be just fine.

Downtown Kempten is not that big, but we are lost, so it seems quite large. We drive back and forth, looking for anything that even resembles a parking space, each time finding that we should have turned and are now heading out of town. After driving over the same bridge for the fifth time, Chris finally gets mad. I have slept well and am in a good mood, which does not help things. I suggest that we pull over and ask, but he feels he is at least smart enough to figure out a town. As we cross over the bridge a sixth time, I enjoy the scenery.

Eventually, I start to worry because my haircut appointment is soon, and we are still on our unintentional driving tour. He says fine, whips the car up a road to our right and we find ourselves barreling toward another vehicle. Both cars stop in time and we wave stupidly as we realize we have driven the wrong way on a one-way street. I am glad to be alive but Chris is mad as hell. He slams it in reverse and guns down the hill, making me cringe in my seat. I think we would have crashed into anyone that had been in the intersection, but luckily, it is empty. I tell him to knock it off and he throws some nice vulgarities my way. I never thought getting a haircut could be so dangerous.

We finally park and walk through the city. Chris wants to wander the streets while I get my haircut. I tell him I will wait for him when I am done as I have already forgotten where the car is parked. I enter the place and ask for Moni. She is the apprentice that will be chopping my hair. Moni comes out from the back room, and three days before our trip is over, I have managed to be smitten one more time.

Moni is adorable, with short black hair and a cute smile. She sits next to me and starts to speak in German. I tell her I am fluent only in English and she can hardly contain her excitement. She has been studying English for ten years, and speaks it better than I do, but makes me promise not to laugh at her mistakes. She offers me some cake and some coffee, I refuse, then ask her if she was aware I have come here for a haircut. She explains that they like to let their customers relax first, and then they discuss their hair and what kind of cut will be working out best for them. She has been cutting hair for over a year and needs six more years to be a master hairdresser.

I tell her I want something that looks casual but sassy, professional yet fun. She looks at my hair and tells me she knows exactly what I need. This kind of confidence I like. She asks me how short I want the sides and I tell her a number three. She has no idea what that means. I tell her that in America, they have the clipper sizes by numbers and that indicates how short you want it. She is shocked that we use clippers at all. She thought only the army used those. She says she learned to cut it all by hand. Anything to keep me here longer is fine with me.

She cuts and we talk. She is my age and looking to move to Paris or America someday. I occasionally look in the mirror and we lock eyes, blush and then look away. It is disgustingly sweet in a high school kind of way. The haircut takes almost an hour, and when she is done, I stand up to look in the big mirror. I look cool. I have a young Elvis/Superman hairdo. She stands between the mirror and me and runs her hands through my hair. Chris sees this through the window and smiles. I try not to look at either one of them.

After I pay the bill, I leave her a tip big enough to lease a car. We talk for a bit and she asks me if I would like to meet for lunch tomorrow. I say I would love to, then I remember I will be on a train to Paris tomorrow. The ideas of postponing our train ride, running away or cutting a day off of Paris all cross my mind. Then it strikes me that right now I have a ton of what ifs in my head, and as the past has shown me, it usually does not get any better than this.

Chris says it is very apparent there was a spark there, and is laughing because I have managed to fall for yet another person on this trip. I defend myself by blaming it on youth, virility, and a large part having to do with survival instinct. He likes my new haircut, it is not falling in my face anymore and he thinks that I look respectable.

We drive to a supermarket and decide to stock up on items to take home. We can only imagine how much more expensive it will be in Paris. We each grab a basket full of Milka chocolate bars and Chris loads up on bag after bag of Gummy Bears. These are for the people back home, or so we tell ourselves as we dig into them on the drive back to the Termonds.

When I walk in the house Christa lets out a squeal. She is excited that she can finally see what my face looks like. I do not think my hair was that long. Chris says that with my short hair and his shaved beard, we have come to Europe as men and are leaving as boys.

Evening is spent talking around the dinner table. This is the last night we will be spending with the family, and though everyone makes plans of future trips, there is really no way of knowing when we will see each other again. Christa hands me a postcard with a name and address on it. It is Moni's. After I returned, Christa called to thank her for the job she did and I think to mention how interested I was in her. Moni told her to tell me goodbye, and gave her address, in case I wanted to write.

We say our good-byes to Bart, Tanja and Brian. They will all be gone by the time we leave tomorrow morning. I fall asleep listening to the sound of the river and the trees tapping against the roof. I am trying to figure out if I will dream about my hair, about Moni or about Chris driving in reverse.

The next morning we wake early and prepare for the train to Paris. It is an eight-hour trip, but at least it is not at night. Our bags are packed and look so much bigger then when we left. Neither of us has bought many things, but I have managed to keep every receipt and brochure that has come my way, and the rocks are now taking up a good space at the bottom. Christa announces it is time for us to go. She is wearing a sport jacket with Levi's and looks fabulous, I cannot wait to get home and wear actual clothes again.

We hop in her BMW and head to the station, and though we are not in a hurry, her car is. I am not looking to forward to saying goodbye to Christa because I have grown to like her so much. We hug for a bit and all seems fine, then I look at her and she is crying. This gives the green flag for my waterworks to begin. The teary-eyed travelers wave goodbye to their equally teary-eyed hostess, and then make their way to track number five for a slow ride to Paris.

A slow ride to Paris, I think that has the makings of a good title for a book, or at least a song. Maybe it could be about lost loves, lost innocence or something or another being lost. We could have a Bob Dylan-type person sing it while strumming a guitar. Then, we could start writing new works, like slow ride to Munich or slow ride to Edinburgh.

Chris is not as enthusiastic as I am about becoming rich in the songwriting industry. He is preoccupied with the fact that the girl sitting next to us went to the restroom, and while she is gone, her orange soda falls over. I am wondering if she will think it is something we did on purpose, Chris is just unhappy that we are now on a crowded train with sticky floors.

During one of our stops, I finally have my own European experience. I have been jealous ever since Chris saw that guy standing to the side of the train tracks with his beret and cigarettes looking like an ad for Europe.

My European Experience: It is a family, a man, a woman and little girl, who run to the door of the car just in front of our rail car. The woman gets on the train with the little girl and the man stands outside their window. The little girl sticks her hand out, reaching for her dad, who takes it gently and kisses it. His wife then puts her hand on the window and he touches the other side of the glass. The train pulls away and he blows them each a kiss. He looks so sad. I turn in my seat and he is still waving at the train. Then I hear the woman talk to her little girl, and even though it is in German, I can hear the emotion in her voice.

CHAPTER EIGHTEEN

Paris

Teacups, Counting Crows and a Boy/Girl

We roll into Paris in the afternoon. Aside from the beautiful countryside of Switzerland and France, the trip is uneventful. The food cart keeps rolling by. The flaky pastries are summoning us, but this is not our fault, they have been purposefully set at eye level. Chris thinks we are being fattened for the market. He says that because all we are doing on this ride is sitting, eating and drinking, the seats have become nothing more than little cattle pens. Then he moos at me.

We pull up to Paris and hop out. Near the train stop is an office that says tourist and hotel information. We assume the best way to find a cheap place to stay is to ask here. There is one lady in the office and she is on the phone. We stand to the side, not wanting to be rude. After ten minutes, she finishes her call and then sits down at her desk. We remain where we are, waiting for her to acknowledge our existence, but to no avail.

Some people come in, a couple that looks like they have money, and they ask her something in French. She shuffles through her papers, gives them a number and then they leave. She returns to ignoring us. I say excuse me and she looks up, making it very obvious that I have bothered her. I tell her that we are looking for a hotel and she tells us she cannot help us. I persist by asking her is this not the hotel and tourist office, to which she rolls her eyes and says there are no hotels to book in the city. Perhaps if we come back later. I am in no mood for this. As we walk out, I say that I hope the rest of Paris is as helpful as she has been. Of course, I already know the answer. She is most likely just the tip of the iceberg.

The first thing we need to do is find the hotel that Gigi told us to stay at. I definitely have problems beyond my medical expertise as we trudge a path away from the station. My feet are beyond hurting and I think that perhaps I somehow stopped my blood circulation during our train trip. I do not remember sitting at any strange angles, or contorting any more than a stretch or a yawn, but all the same, there are troubles brewing. Adding to this is the fact that Chris is trying to find the hotel by walking somewhere between haphazardly and aimlessly.

The streets should be going from left to right, or at least east to west, but they are not. The streets of Paris are in a circle, a square and a couple of octagons. They cross to the left, the right and diagonally, and we follow them. I cannot believe how hard it would be just to stop and ask for directions. This is not an I.Q. test. People are not judging our smarts on whether or not we can navigate a city that was built by Germanic Hordes, we need only to pull over and ask. But we do not. Instead, we walk for miles on end. I finally take it upon myself to berate Chris with my feelings toward him. Of course, by this point he is already half a block ahead of me, so I have to shout and catch up, to the amusement of the French onlookers.

Thirteen years later, still searching for our hotel, I trip on a piece of uneven sidewalk. It is not a fall down type of trip, but the kind that forces you to jog a few steps and then look back at the inanimate item that really had nothing to do with your clumsiness. We walk in silence for a bit and then I explode. "I cannot believe you did not even ask me if I was okay," I yell at him. "I could have been seriously injured."

He stares straight ahead and says nothing. I know I am overreacting by this point, but I almost fell to my death and he does not so much as blink his left eye. That is what spending every day of every week with someone amounts to, apathy, how sweet.

I decide to get over my anger and then do. It is so much easier for me to control my anger these days, especially when I cannot remember why I have gotten mad. We get to the hotel and they are booked up. They suggest one down the street and off we go. This one is booked too. However, the man at the desk calls another hotel, and they have a room, so he takes us there. For being French, he is incredibly helpful. He must not have gotten the memo.

The hotel is a dingy looking building, with a front door we can hardly squeeze through. Chris is a good deal thinner than I am and even he has trouble. Of course, if I were unable to make it through the door I would bet money that he would leave me outside. The hallway is no bigger than the door, but the grime on the walls has a certain charm to it.

At the front desk is this kid with a crew cut, and we cannot tell if it is a he or a she. This kid-thing is wearing a white curtain-type dress with a flower on the front. It looks like a kid-size moo moo. Our escort tells it what we want and leaves. The kid-thing looks at us for a good two minutes and then grabs a key off the wall as it heads out the office door.

As we are climbing the four flights of stairs, I ask Chris if that is a boy or a girl. He says he cannot tell because of the extra-short haircut, which by the way he hates because they come off as too practical and icy looking, especially on women. The kid-thing is not within earshot of our conversation. It is instead hurtling itself up the stairs and singing something in French.

When we reach our floor, it continues to sing its song, looking back at us to make sure we are following. We get to the door and it unlocks it, faces us and continues singing the song. At the end of the performance, the kid-thing does a pathetically loud yell and karate chops open our door. I can only imagine how many times it was dropped on its head as a youngster.

The room is dingy and gross, with a window that faces into another window ten feet away. The beds are fifty years old and the sheets look like Moses could have once used them. Off to the right is a shower that sticks halfway into the room. The one light bulb barely lights the room, throwing everything is shadows, which is probably a good thing. The little, dress wearing kid-thing plops itself on the bed Chris has chosen. I go to see what color the shower water is.

When I turn around, the kid-thing is on my bed, the dress is up a little and I can see one of its butt cheeks touching my bedspread. I tell the little creep to get off, but it rubs together its thumb and forefinger. Nice, teach them young, the little bastard. I give it a ten-franc and it scampers off my bed. Chris asks it where the toilet is and it motions him to follow, walking back down the hall, continuing the song where it left off.

When Chris gets back, he says that the little creature decided to finish its song while holding its dress above its head. Having on no underwear, Chris can safely say that the illegitimate freak was in fact a boy. I am only glad our host took his naked ass off my bedspread and it only cost me ten francs. Chris is shocked. He did the same thing to him and he also gave him ten francs. I am thinking that is not bad for two minutes of actual work. The little guy should be proud. Maybe he should buy himself a new dress or something.

We decide immediately to leave the room and go out. We can sleep here but they cannot make us experience it fully awake. I rig up the backpacks so that they are not only padlocked to each other and the fifty-year old bed frame, but are also balanced in a way that will ensure they will crush any smaller people that mess with them. I am willing to bet money our lunatic-bellboy ransacks rooms on a daily basis, singing to, karate chopping and rubbing his bare bottom on the items left behind.

We walk the city and look at the sights. As night approaches, the Seine is a deep purple, soaking up the light from lanterns on its banks. Across the river, the Eiffel Tower lights up and I now feel like I am in Paris. We walk for a while trying to find a place to eat. We are not in the mood for a big meal, but all the menus posted outside seem to offer only wares for the starving tourist. Around the corner, we hear some music, and then we see a familiar sight. It is a Hard Rock Café.

I have been to them all over America and the one in Amsterdam too, so I tell Chris I need to go in here and buy myself a hat. We wander in and instantly catch the smell of hamburgers grilling, fries frying and Coke fizzing. One shared look and we head for the dining room, to enjoy an American meal in Paris. The waitress is American, the food is greasy and the music is loud. Within ten minutes, we feel like we are back home. I am not proud that we are doing this, but any guilt I have disappears with the first bite of my juicy hamburger.

We walk to the Eiffel Tower and then the Arch de Triomphe. Everything is bathed in white lights. I cannot understand why we do not take the time to light up buildings back home, but I guess the ambience would be lost when you would see a Taco Bell glowing softly in the night. Chris thinks we need to see the river at night, but the only things that we can see are the blinding lights of the tourist boats as they chug up and down the water.

Finally, it is late enough and we are tired enough to not care how bad our hotel room looks. We go back and head up the four flights of stairs. As we are trying to fit the key in the door, the little dress wearing, chimp-boy runs around the corner, stops and gives us the evil eye. Chris says he is a shoe-in for a David Lynch casting call.

The next morning we head downstairs to reserve the room for another night. We hate this place, but everywhere else appears booked. Our friend the kid is not at the desk, instead it is his father, a rough-looking old guy. We tell him that we want to pay for another night and show him our key with the room number on it. He shakes his head no. Apparently, he has a wedding party coming in that has reserved all of the rooms. We ask him if he has any open rooms and he says no, and tells us to please take our things and go. Luckily I am a morning person or this would really be making me mad right now.

We head over to the hotel that we tried first, thinking perhaps a room has opened up, but this did not happen. A woman at the counter makes a call and tells us to go to this place at that place. She is talking in French and we understand English, so we stare at her in the hopes that something more will happen. Our plan works and she becomes annoyed. She gets up and heads into the street, motioning us to follow her. She is an older lady with a square body and looks like she likes to kill her own dinners. We try to keep up with her, but she is doing some sort of army march that she apparently acquired in her youth and we are running to keep up. She stops at one point to buy a baguette, but then carries it slung over her shoulder like a rifle, confirming my earlier thoughts of a past enlistment.

We arrive at what looks to someday be a very nice hotel, but for now, a lot of scaffolding and paint tarps. We thank the lady and she bows to us, rifle/baguette at her side. Walking in, the smell makes Chris think of a paint store, I can only wonder if everyone knows not to light a match in here. The man behind the counter is happy to see us.

The hotel has just opened and we are his first guests. The cost is somewhere around thirty dollars each. I ask him if being his first guests entitles us to any sort of first-guest discount. He laughs and shakes his head no, and then he asks if he can borrow my pen. He has nothing at the front desk to write with, which is not his fault, because the front desk is not quite built yet. Chris is just happy that there are no naked French kids dancing around.

Our room is immaculate and there is a certain excitement that accompanies knowing that no one has ever touched these things before. We happily remove the plastic off the toilet seat, the hairdryer and the remote control. The bed sheets are so crisp they hurt and the walls are so white they shimmer. The television is mounted to the wall, much like in a hospital room, and I immediately grab the bed that faces the device I have missed most of all.

We decide that today we will go to EuroDisney. For some reason, we seem to be putting off the city of Paris. I wonder if it is because it is the last one and we do not want to admit the trip is close to being over, or if we are just tired of looking at marble, churches and six hundred year old things that have postcard carts outside. Chris is excited to go because the Disneyland in Paris has an Indiana Jones ride that the States have not yet built. I am excited to go because I will finally be able to use my credit card.

Finding EuroDisney is the easiest thing in the world. The signs point to where we need to go, the subway takes us straight there and the conductor announces when we have arrived. The land of enchantment is outside of Paris, but close enough to not be an annoying trip. We are excited at the fact that we keep hearing that this theme park is failing miserably. That should mean no long lines for the rides.

Walking to the park entrance makes us feel like little kids. There is a big sign welcoming us, behind that we can see a castle and further back, people hurtling around on various contraptions. The only thing that shatters these dreams of my childhood is the ticket lady, who charges me forty-five dollars to get in. As a kid, I did not even know it cost anything to get in, thinking that was why everyone called it the happiest place on earth. Oh how I miss the innocence of youth.

First, we hit the Star Wars ride. There is a full-scale model of an X-wing fighter in front, which already outdoes what they have in California. We sit down for the show, and Chris is fascinated with the fact that C-3PO speaks French. He says that he knew that this robot spoke over six million languages, but for some reason he never thought one of these would be French. After this, we head to the Indiana Jones roller coaster, and its interesting loop, which you make while upside down. I clock the total ride time at around forty-nine seconds, which is not much considering we have been standing in line for over an hour.

After this, we go to Pirates of the Caribbean, which has us walking through a maze of pirate dungeons to get there. Though French is a romantic language, when grunted and spat at you by a man in dire need of a shave, it comes off as a bit frightening. The pirates are rugged and the ride is fun, except for the first part that took us past the windows of a dining room. Watching people eat overpriced lobster is not a very nautical experience. When the ride ends, we are so impressed we head to the pirate store and buy rag hats. We look like idiots wearing our pirate hats, but the chance of running into anyone we know is quite minimal.

Now it's on to the teacup ride. I have never understood this ride, but Chris seems excited so we go. We sit in the cup and the whole contraption starts to spin. In the middle of the teacup is a small, metal table, which you turn to make your cup go around faster. Chris is pulling at this and we are spinning. The faster he turns it the faster we spin. Up to a certain speed, I tell him to knock it off. I can feel the nausea coming on. He says something about me being wimpy and turns it faster. I warn him to stop, but he keeps on.

Finally I snap and tell him that if he wants to spin, then dammit, we shall spin. I grab the metal disk and turn it with all my might. We are spinning so fast the people on the side look like they are vertical. Eventually the ride stops, but we are unable to focus enough to find the exit. I stumble out of the cup and head toward the direction I see other people going. My eyes are still fixed on the exit but my legs have taken me twenty feet to the left of it. I try again and do no better. I have an incredible urge to drop on all fours and crawl. Finally, I grab the railing on the side and guide myself out.

We go to a bench and sit down. The world is still spinning and I notice that we are both sitting at a forty-five degree angle. Straightening myself brings on nausea, so I remain slanted. After ten minutes, the spinning stops, but the nausea decides to linger for a bit. I am finally able to walk, but feeling like I am carsick with a nice sprinkling of seasickness to go with it. We go towards the other side of the park and Chris stops to buy some popcorn. Watching him shovel the kernels into his mouth almost makes me throw up.

We stop at a change booth because Chris needs to turn the rest of his money into francs. I finally see him fall head over heels for someone. The girl at the change booth is sweet, with long brown hair and an English accent. She goes back to the safe and he leans over to me but says nothing. His eyes are wide and his smile is goofy. The poor boy is in love. I am wondering if he is going to want to come here to change money during the rest of our Paris stay.

As our last ride, we get on the train that circles the park. The one in California takes you through the Grand Canyon and dinosaur country. This one does not do much of anything. We finally hop off in Frontier Land. Chris notices that they are playing the theme song to The Magnificent Seven, and says this is a wonderful exiting song as we leave the park. We decide that whoever said that EuroDisney is failing is full of crap. No ride took less than an hour in line. Though one thing that is interesting, we did run into more Americans here than anywhere else. I guess it is the happiest place on earth, at least for Americans anyway.

The ride back to Paris is quick, but I still manage to feel queasy near the end. I do not think I have fully recovered from those teacups. It is dark when we roll into town and we are only thinking about eating and sleeping. We head to a restaurant and eat steaks and frittes. The waiter is not as pretentious as I expected, but he does manage to come off as an ass. The coffee is marvelous in its own right, but being able to sit and stare out onto a Parisian street makes it taste that much smoother. After walking around the city for a while longer, we decide to call it a night.

We wake up rested but tired. We slept well, but the sheer exhaustion of traveling seems to be something we are unable to shake off so easily. We walk to a café and indulge in coffee and a croissant. I am actually in the mood for another treat I see behind the counter glass, but the lady is unwilling to bend low enough to see what I am pointing at. Trying to pronounce it does no good, so I finally give up and asked for a croissant.

I have a thought about the difference we are experiencing between the French and the Italians. In Italy, all you have to do is attempt to speak the language, and they are excited that you have made an effort and are happy to help you. In France, the words can be pronounced near perfect, but if there is an emphasis put on the wrong word, or a sound is held to long, they will do their best to make you feel like an incompetent. It seems that the Italians want to share those things which make them unique in the world; the French want to conceal theirs.

We walk to the Eiffel Tower, which is impressive from far away, and gigantic up close. Chris notices that the tower is not black, but actually brown. I notice that the lines are at least a mile long. We count our money and realize that we do not have enough to go up. We spent everything at EuroDisney because we are children. Instead, we eat cheese sandwiches under the Eiffel tower and I stagger around looking for a rock to add to my collection. We cross the Seine on the pont d'Iéna and climb the stairs of the place du Trocadéro.

Despite the view of the Eiffel Tower, the fountains and the statues that line the mall, we find our attention focused on the skaters. At least twenty guys and girls are on in-line skates, and they are doing the most amazing stunts for the tourists. We see back flips, front flips and people jumping over each other. Then, to top it off, they race straight down a huge stairway. This last part scares me. Not because I think one of them may die, but because I do not know how to say, apply pressure here, in French. Chris takes a picture of me that looks like I am as big as the Eiffel Tower and then we go.

Next is the Arc de Triomphe. The monument itself is on a stone slab that sits in the middle of traffic. Thirteen roads converge into a circle that goes around the monument. We see people at the monument and we see people on this side, but how we get over there, we do not know. I suppose we cross the street.

At first, it seems easy. The cars are coming from the left, and each is merging to the right, so if we keep our eyes to the left and step ahead of the cars coming toward us, we should be fine. Luckily, there seems to be a slowing in traffic and we make it across. I am impressed we did not even get honked at. We look at the monument and read all the inscriptions. Chris wants to go to the top, but a sign says the stairwell is closed until evening. He is especially impressed with this place and says there is something about large chunks of concrete that always get to him.

We decide to head back and I notice a lot of old people walking around. The traffic is whizzing by and I cannot figure out exactly how they got across here. Then I see it. A stairwell leading underground, to a walkway, which is what we were supposed to use to get here. We walk to the underground sidewalk and listen to a man play the flute for us. When we reach the other side, I stop and watch the traffic go by. The seemingly reckless driving is raising my blood pressure. Now that I know we were not supposed to cross the way we did, it all seems so frightening and deadly. Just seeing what speeds the cars are going around is making me dizzy. I would not try that again if you paid me.

We stop at a restroom not far from the Arc. While standing at the urinal, I notice the guy to my right is throwing angry looks across the room. I do not want him to know I have seen him do this, so I remain focused on the job at hand. When I go to wash my hands, I look to where he was glaring. Standing at a urinal is an older gentleman of sixty or so years. He looks to be urinating, but also watching those around him. As I leave I glance at him again, and notice that he not urinating, he is in fact rubbing himself. I do not know if Chris saw him, but decide it best not to tell him. The poor boy has enough to worry about without thinking he may have been the object of an older gentleman's fantasy.

We walk down the Champs-Elysées. The street is full of people and it is obvious the tourist business is booming. We see a McDonalds, but do not go in. Instead, we head to the Place de la Concorde, to where large groups of people are gathered.

There is a wedding coming to an end, and the happy couple is posing on a Harley near the obelisk. Behind them is a beautiful American car from the 1960's. Chris thinks his photo of the couple, the car and the obelisk is priceless. He will title this picture, *Detroit's finest and a monument from 33 BC.*

We walk back through the park area and find a fountain with chairs around it. The fountain is nothing to brag about, merely a round pond with a pipe in the middle which spurts up water. The chairs are also nothing to write home about, small, uncomfortable and few. We must sit though. Chris says Paris is the city where people sit a lot. After we watch the people walk by and see the characters that occupy the other chairs, this slowly becomes the best place for us to be. Chris is feeling contemplative as he reflects upon the day, the city and the trip. I am wondering why these people do not clean up after their dogs. The fountain spurts away.

On to Notre-Dame, the church of churches. We both immediately notice that it is not as impressive as we had thought, but this can only be blamed on the fact that the last church we saw was St. Peter's, and because the entire front is covered in scaffolding. It looks like a church in a giant cage. The inside is very impressive, but the constant shushing of the other visitors is pretty annoying. We cattle-walk our way around with the other meat and eventually make our way out. Chris was especially impressed with the flying buttresses, while I thought the giant window had some good points to it.

We did not make it to the top of the Eiffel Tower, the Arc de Triomphe was not open and now the top part of Notre-Dame is closed. I am thinking this is some sort of French conspiracy. We cross the river and enter the Shakespeare & Co. Bookstore. The store is impossibly crowded and any chance of finding something specific is near impossible. The owner looks to be straight out of a Dickens novel. Chris thinks he looks like a crusty, old British guy. The only book I find I want to buy is The Little Prince, but the price is a few francs above astronomical. Chris finds many copies of A Moveable Feast, but he cannot see paying sixty francs for a three-dollar paperback. It is a memorable experience none the less, and stopping in to soak up the ambience is well worth the stop.

We walk around the Latin Quarter and as evening descends we are both wishing the other is not who the other is. This, like Venice, is a city for lovers. Along the Seine, we see houseboats tied for the night and the sound of music and laughing floats up to us. I read once that William Wharton lives on one of these boats. I daydream about running into him and talking books, I wonder if he is watching me right now and daydreaming about running into me and talking about books. Well, you never know.

Night descends and we work our way back to the hotel. The glass pyramid outside of the Louvre glows for our enjoyment and Chris takes this as a sign to come visit the museum tomorrow. We lose sight of the Eiffel Tower and I am immediately lost again. I decide to let Chris find the way back as I keep an eye out for muggers and French ladies, not necessarily in that order.

The next morning we awaken to the sound of construction. Chris is going to the Louvre, I decide that I am not. Last night I was thinking that I am tired of cramming everything into one day, and today we only have a couple of hours before we have to be at the airport. Chris is planning on running in and seeing the big attractions, mainly the Mona Lisa, the Venus de Milo and a few other works. I figure I will be back one day and would rather take my time in there. There are Michelangelo's and Pannini's that should not be rushed.

I am also tired of hanging out with him, not in a mean way, but it is true. I know he feels the same way, but we have been very civil about it. I am not tired of him as a person. I still like him. I just want to put some space between us for a bit. I am impressed at the amount of kindness he has shown me, being that I am ten times more annoying than he is. He tells me he will be back in an hour and heads off to experience art. I sit in my bed and turn on European MTV. There is an Erasure video on and I sing along.

The MTV guy announces that the Counting Crows are in Paris, not on tour, but just hanging out to get away from it all. I decide that this must be a sign and go out to find my illusive Crows. I try to keep track of my right turns and left turns but twenty minutes later I am lost. I remember how to get back by following the major attractions, so unless they tear down the Eiffel Tower within the next hour, I should be okay. I reach a park that has a courtyard to one side. In the courtyard, I see a head I recognize. It is large, stone and tilted to the side. A huge, stone hand sits next to it. This is the head that they used in the movie Sabrina.

Some ruffian has taken to adding red spray paint to the lips, but it still makes for a wonderful picture. I only wish Chris were here to take it so that I could place my body in the palm of the hand. I take my photos and notice two creepy looking guys in black jackets are walking towards me, but not in a normal approaching way, more in the making sure no one else is around type of way. I head to safer ground and walk the streets for a while.

The Seine is full of tourists and the artists are selling their works. Each artist has an amazing picture or two to sell, but oddly, they all look similar. Did they all go to the same school? Do they teach one another? Have the French developed a really good color copier? I walk for a while longer, stop in a café for a coffee and see a man that looks like Roald Dahl ordering a sandwich. I thought he was dead, but maybe he just moved to Paris, either way I decide not to bother him. I eventually return to the hotel, as does Chris. We pack up our bags to leave.

We check out and the man behind the near-completed front desk asks if we enjoyed our stay. We tell him that the place seems to be coming along nicely and the toilet paper remained well stocked. We have only good things to say about this place. He does not hear any of this though. He is too busy looking for a pen to sign us out with.

On the way to the airport Chris tells me that the Louvre was much more impressive than he thought it would be. It is modern and spacious inside, and because he went early, he had only three other people looking at the Mona Lisa with him. I decide not to tell him that I spent my time almost getting mugged and searching for the Counting Crows.

With the little money we have left, we stock up on candy and magazines for the trip. Our bags are too heavy to stick in our overhead compartments, something we were able to get away with on the way here, though I cannot figure how we did it. We are set to fly into Cincinnati and then to Phoenix, assuming we are on the right plane. I stopped paying attention after the ticket lady scolded me for not having my passport ready.

Paris is the city of lights, lovers and great coffee. The river is magical and the streets are impressive. I just hope that someone lets the people know that their rudeness is coming very close to bypassing Lacrosse as their national sport. Then again, if it were any other way, it would lose some of its charm.

CHAPTER NINETEEN

Return

Customs, Partial Fatherhood and a Mad Dash for Home

I am nervous because our plane has a go-down number. Flight 146 out of Paris. It just reeks of disaster. You never hear flight 14 or flight 145 and 1/8th careened into the ocean, but numbers like 405, 292, and 146 are always finding a way to show their passengers what the bottom of the Atlantic looks like. I may as well kiss my young ass goodbye.

Our flight is a strange one. We are leaving Paris in the early afternoon and arriving in the states sometime in early afternoon. This should make for some interesting jet lag. The seats have somehow shrunk since the last time I flew, and I wonder if this is the next step in the aviation industries attempt to make me want to fly more. Of course, they know I will be paying to fly no matter what they do to me, my only other choice being a three month boat ride that would promise an abundance of hunger and small pox.

They give each of us a bag. It is supposed to contain everything we need to conquer our lunchtime hunger. I think its amazing what airlines can get away with these days. The price you pay for a ticket should get you wined and dined, and for the price of a first class seat, they should at least provide entertainment in the form of juggling or perhaps a small magic show. Instead, I am eating a dry sandwich out of a paper bag and washing it down with miniature bottles of whiskey.

That is the only positive about international flights. You get free booze. I ask the stewardess for two bottles and then the next stewardess for two more. I hope to arrive home with enough miniature bottles to open a miniature bar. Maybe I can even have the added amusement of eighty-sixing miniature winos every now and then.

We have somehow managed to score the seats in the front of the middle section. The legroom is amazing. I can almost stretch them halfway. The only drawback is that the movie screen is now right directly in front of us. Chris does not have to contend with huge-headed passengers blocking his view, but now we have to watch the acting nuances of nostrils.

The seat next to me is empty and the stewardess lets a woman with a baby sit here. I do not really foresee any problems with this, as long as the baby knows how to keep it down during pivotal parts of the film. We are watching The Pelican Brief, which I find more entertaining when I take off my headphones. Afterwards the lady decides it is time to feed the child, and though she is an attractive new mother, I respectfully stare at the exit door in the opposite direction the entire time her breast makes its appearance.

Hours later and another meal is served. This one requires the use of forks and knives and smells like it was reheated with petrol. I decide to forego this meal and then notice that the woman is having a hard time eating and holding her offspring. I offer to take the kid, which she laughs off as a ridiculous idea and continues to juggle. Not wanting to hear the cries of a freshly dropped child, I tell her that I am serious, I would not mind. She thinks about it for a minute and then says if it really is not too much trouble. I tell her it is not and my prize is a kid.

It is a small thing, barely a head and some legs, though I am sure the rest of it is huddling in there somewhere. Barely awake, it gurgles a bit, makes as if to swat off its nose and then falls back asleep. The mother eats her meal and then offers to take the kid back, I can tell she feels guilty. I tell her that the kid and I are both comfortable, if she needs to go to the bathroom or anything. Without a second to lose, she jumps at the chance and heads to the water closet.

When she gets back, I notice how red her eyes are. She is also yawning uncontrollably. I tell her that I cannot sleep on flights, so if she wants to take a nap, the kid and I will just hang out. She feels too guilty to do this, but I ask her when the last time she slept was and she looks at me sheepishly. I have to promise to wake her if I want to give the kid back, no matter what. She curls up to sleep and I watch the baby and its mom dream and drool.

One would think that some sort of fatherly instinct would take over at this point and I would start thinking about when I can have one of my own. In all honesty, I am only too glad to know that I will be giving this tiny human back soon and will be able to go on my way. At this point, I do not even have the urge to care for a dog, much less a person that cannot control its bowel movements.

I usually like to spend airplane time catching up on my reading, but I am still a little nauseous from the teacups. The baby sleeps, gurgles and drools. I sit, gurgle and yawn. Eventually the mother wakes up and takes the little guy from me. She has napped for almost two hours and looks so much better for it. She thanks me and tells me what a nice man I am. I just feel bad that she will probably not sleep like that again until the kid leaves home for college.

They announce that we are close to our destination by bringing out the little, steaming towels. The stewardess hands it to me with tongs and says be careful, it is hot. As I grab this inferno with my bare hands to slap in on my bare face, I thank her for the warning. I wonder what the people in first class get at this point. Surely not pathetically, soggy hand towels, which have been in the microwave too long. Maybe they get soggy robes to put on, or at least large, wet towels, or maybe a hot oil rubdown. That would explain letting them off the plane first. It would keep us from seeing the looks of ecstasy on their faces.

The plane makes an extraordinarily hard landing and eventually rolls to a stop. The people around us explode with applause. Why they would clap for such a discomforting landing is beyond me, then again, this could just be a way of saying thank you for not killing us today. The captain thanks us for flying and I swear he is slurring his words more then when the flight began. The stewardess tells everyone to remain seated until the plane has come to a complete stop, but I miss part of her message as I dodge bodies trying to wrestle their bags out of the overhead bins.

We get off the plane and go through customs. The guy looking at my passport must be tired today. He asks me how long I will be in the states and I tell him I will most likely be buried here. He realizes he is not in the foreign passport line and tells me to keep the line moving. We are told that we need to get our bags and then recheck through customs. They give us the number of the baggage carousel and we begin our journey.

Cincinnati airport was boring the first time we were here and our second visit shows us that we were not wrong the first time. At least in Detroit they show their pride by having cars parked in the middle of the airport, like a showroom. Of course, maybe Cincinnati is not known for producing anything as cool as automobiles. They may have the misfortune of being the feminine hygiene manufacturer of the country, or worse yet, the makers of suppositories. Not that either of these things are to be ashamed of, they just do not make for very good airport lobby decorations.

We make it to the baggage carousel, which is conveniently located thirty-six miles from where the plane disembarked. Luckily, we have a two-hour layover and the airport has many moving sidewalks. We glide our way there. Seeing other people from our plane assures us we are in the right area, and then our plane number flashes on the screen. Bags begin to pour out. There are big ones, little ones, black ones and brown ones. Every bag seems to be represented on this carousel, every bag except ours.

We go to the customer service lady, who tells us that our bags should be arriving, so we can recheck them through customs. We tell her that is what we were told, but they did not arrive with the rest of the bags. She answers us with a super-intelligent shrug of the shoulders. Some bags take longer to unload, she says, so they will probably show up. I wonder if the fact that our bags look like we are transporting bodies has caused some confusion. Maybe someone has stumbled upon my rocks. Anything could have gone wrong, which reminds me how bad I am at making myself feel better. We put on our lost puppy faces and sit down next to the carousel. Maybe our bags are just taking a little longer to unload, yeah right!

We talk, eat, nap and sing. At one point, we even contemplate starting a campfire, but neither of us has matches and the marshmallows are in my bag. Chris leisurely looks at his watch and notices that time somehow flew by without our knowledge. We have fifteen minutes before out flight for

Phoenix leaves. I go to customer service again, and this time it is a different lady behind the counter. I tell her we are waiting for our bags and she punches some keys on a keyboard. Apparently the other lady has not been trained on the computer yet, or customer service, or the ability to communicate. She tells us that for some reason our bags have been routed to Phoenix, and are already on the plane. The same plane that we have to be on within the next thirteen minutes.

I run by where Chris is sitting and yell at him to follow me. He asks me why, but I have no time for small talk. The thought of being trapped in Cincinnati is scaring the hell out of me. Having a running conversation, I tell him that our bags are going to Phoenix without us. We make a mad dash through the airport.

The teamwork of yesteryear kicks in and we move as a well-oiled machine. He is running ahead of me, and being thin, jumps between people in our way. After clearing these obstacles, he yells excuse me, which makes them instinctively move aside, just wide enough for me to barrel through. We dash around families, race against carts and at one time I think I jump over a child, but this could be the adrenaline reminding me of a movie I once saw. I yell out the terminal letter and he leads us there. I shout out the gate number and we torpedo into the waiting area. The metal door has not yet shut and we almost run into it full speed. We make it with a minute and a half to spare. As we settle in our seats, we are both glowing with perspiration and pride. The city of Cincinnati is not able to claim two more victims this day.

Chris takes a nap and I look through the airplane magazines. This is our last use of public transportation unless our rides forget to pick us up at the airport. I am trying to write something meaningful and profound in my journal, but I cannot think of anything interesting to say. I write down what I liked most in each city and this only helps to make me sad. I think about the train ride through Scotland and the hills of Edinburgh. The city view of Florence when we thought we were lost. Being able to see Placido Domingo in Vienna and having a beer fight in Amsterdam. The Van Gogh museum, confessing in St. Peters and the friends we made in Nottingham. There was Dachua, the ringing of the bells in Prague and the girl who cut my hair. The Termonds, the woman at the party and the boat parade in Venice.

These all come out in a haphazard order and I can only list them one after the other. I am unable to explain what each one means to me. Some are funny, some were stupid and a few were simply magical. I cannot sum up much of anything. I have not made any revelations about life and I feel no closer to having an answer to anything. On the other hand, I feel like I have done something important and it will change the way I look at things from now on. Europe has shown me that the earth is a big place, but the world is a small one. The airplane is circling to land and I have one more page to fill in my journal. On the first page of my journal, I had written the following:

Unable to grasp my existence at this point in life, I have decided to take a trip to find meaning. I have been told that one cannot find meaning in places or things, but only in oneself. So, I take this trip in search of myself.

I could not have sounded more depressing if I had tried. Chris says that I take some things a little too seriously, even when I try to look like I have not a care in the world. I cannot say that I have found the answer to this crusade I set for myself. I cannot even say that I understand what the hell it means anymore. The plane is taxing and there is only one thing I can remember that seems to fit what I am feeling right now, so I write it down. It is a quote from Michner. He said: *Men ought to inspect their dreams, and know them for what they are.*

EPILOGUE

When we landed in Phoenix, we hugged our families and found our luggage. I suppose one could also say that we found our families and hugged our luggage. After so long together we had nothing to say to each other, so we each gave the other a small wave and went to our respective homes. We did not talk for over a month, nor did either one of us tell others about the trip. I think we both needed some time to let it all soak in.

Since then, I have read both of our travel journals. Chris had the more accurate one, but it was incredibly carefree and funny. Mine was filled with deep thoughts about nothing and half-thoughts sprinkled with half-truths. Many of the places still stick in my memory, but the faces of people are fading. I wrote to Moni, the hairdresser, for a few months, but we eventually lost touch. The Termonds I keep in contact with.

I see little pieces of Europe all around me and I think, in a way, they are what keep me going. Driving once through Napa Valley, I was suddenly in the hills of Scotland. Heavy fog in Seattle reminded me of London or York and the river in Portland often took me back to a stroll in Inverness. I am still unable to spin in an office chair without getting nauseous, but I am starting to accept that this is less the teacup's fault and more my own.

Chris says that ever since the trip, people and places seem to mean much more to him. Perhaps it showed us that there is beauty in the world and we are never too old to learn new things. Maybe it helped us to see that we are all not as different as we like to think we are. Or maybe, just like me, he is just waiting for the chance to do it all again.

I did make it back to the Accademia in Florence, and seeing David was worth every penny of the trip. The Notre-Dame was also open this time, as was the Arc de Triomphe. I also had enough money to go to the top of the Eiffel Tower. The Louvre was as fancy as Chris said it was and I figured out how to make money come out of an ATM in Monaco. There have been many more adventures since this one came to an end. Those, however, I will save for another time.

-END-